Northern
Breakthrough

Wadsworth Publishing Company, Inc., Belmont, California

Northern Breakthrough

Robert O. Blood, Jr.
The University of Michigan

Preface

This book is the record of a natural field experiment in fair employment within the key retail stores of the northern metropolis of Minneapolis and St. Paul. The book is a case study in social change — the elements of resistance and the agencies, the strategies, and the consequences of change. Its purpose is to increase our understanding of social and social-psychological processes through the analysis of the forces at work in a particular community at a critical time. As a case study, this book contributes historical depth to sociological analysis. Written primarily for the undergraduate student, this research monograph is designed for supplementary reading in courses in race relations, social problems, social change, social psychology, and business management.

The book begins with an analysis of the status quo of discriminatory employment. It then analyzes the experiences of those stores that pioneered in employing the first Negro salesgirls and office workers in the history of Minneapolis and St. Paul. These kinds of experiences are compared with the personnel managers' prior predictions of Negro job performance, white employee reactions, and white customer reactions. The prior predictions of those managers who were experienced with Negro personnel are also compared with the predictions of the managers who had yet to employ their first Negro above the job ceiling.

The second half of the book analyzes the forces responsible for these employment breakthroughs. A search for personal prejudice in the managers leads to a re-examination of the relationship between discrimination and prejudice. Particular attention is paid to the role of pressure groups in initiating new employment practices. The book also explores from the managers' point of view the controversial issue of government intervention in employment practices. The concluding chapter traces the escalation of Negro-white conflict since the time of this study.

Interviews with the personnel managers or top executives of the 50 largest stores in Minneapolis and St. Paul provided the basic data for this case study. The research method is presented in the Appendix along with the text of the Minneapolis Fair Employment Practices ordinance and a comparative analysis of other F.E.P.C. laws of similar vintage.

The following executives of five metropolitan human-relations organizations shared their practical experience in promoting racial integration (and also provided copies of written materials as well as access to their files and use of their offices in arranging interviews with the store managers): Whitney M. Young, Jr., of the St. Paul Urban League (now executive director of the National Urban League); S. Vincent Owens, also of the St. Paul Urban League; William Seabron, of the Minneapolis Urban League; Wilfred C. Leland, Jr., of the Minneapolis Fair Employment Practices Commission; Frank W. Fager, of the Minneapolis Mayor's Council on Human Relations; and Samuel L. Scheiner, of the Jewish Community Relations Council of Minnesota.

This study was executed in consultation with Professor Theodore Caplow, of Columbia University, and Professor Arnold Rose, of the University of Minnesota. I am indebted to the careful and critical reviews of the draft manuscript by Professors John Leggett, of Simon Fraser University (British Columbia), and Thomas Pettigrew, of Harvard University. Although they should not be held responsible for deficiencies that the reader may find in the text, these reviewers have contributed many suggestions, some of which I have quoted explicitly.

Robert O. Blood, Jr.

Contents

List of Tables

List of Figures

Figure

Part 1
Northern Breakthrough

The first half of the book compares what people thought would happen when the first Negroes broke through the retail job ceiling in the Twin Cities with what actually happened. It is a study in prophecy and fulfillment, myth and reality.

Chapter 1

The North on the Brink of Change

The 1940s are a long time ago in the history of American race relations. But they were crucial years. During World War II, the Federal Government established the first Fair Employment Practices Commission this country ever had. Spurred by wartime labor shortages, Negroes moved into new jobs in war production. Negro soldiers overseas enjoyed the taste of freedom in color-blind countries. The army experimented with mixed units of Negro and white soldiers. Change was in the air and democracy was its battle cry.

When the war ended, the munitions factories closed, and Negroes lost their jobs. No longer sustained by a war emergency, the F.E.P.C. died. Change slipped into reverse. But for Negro veterans, the impetus to progress was greater than ever. Reversals on the home front betrayed wartime promises. Men who had seen "Paree" were hardly prepared to return to the ghetto. Moreover, Army training and the postwar GI bill qualified thousands of men better than ever before for jobs they had traditionally been denied.

The postwar reverses and the war-born forces clashed head on. The net result was an upsurge of the civil-rights movement. It is difficult to say exactly when the civil-rights movement began. In some ways it is the modern successor to the slave revolts of the plantation era. Thomas Pettigrew points out that many of the conditions following World War II echoed those that existed after World War I, yet conditions were not ripe then for the movement to catch fire. In the meantime, masses of American Negroes moved from feudal rural counties to more explosive urban areas. The C.I.O. organized thousands into militant labor unions. The New Deal enhanced the role of government on behalf of the poor. These are at least some of the factors that made American Negroes less prepared to resume their prewar status in the 1940s than they had been in the 1920s.

A major objective of the movement was fair employment. Between 1945 and 1947, four states and three cities passed fair-employment laws to replace the federal commission (see Appendix). In northern cities with and without such laws, the campaign for fair employment shifted from the arsenals of war to the commerce of peace. Retail stores became a prime target of attack.

3

The Twin Cities of Minneapolis and St. Paul were one battleground in that campaign. These northernmost big cities in the United States exhibited employment patterns almost as segregated as Atlanta's. Most Negroes worked in "Negro jobs"—janitors and ditch diggers, maids and laundry workers. White-collar jobs were lily-white. With the rarest exceptions, no Negro had ever stood behind the sales counter of a downtown store. Nor were any downtown offices integrated, save for governmental and reform organizations. Yet change was in the air, and old barriers could not hold forever.

The late 1940s were breakthrough years in the Twin Cities. In 1947 Minneapolis passed a Fair Employment Practices ordinance. In 1948 major department stores in both cities gingerly hired their first Negro salesgirls.

The first new jobs are always the hardest to get. Once the dike is breached, the hole widens. The first breakthroughs are also the most interesting to watch. They yield comparisons between advance predictions and actual happenings, and they provide a natural experiment in the causes and effects of social change.

In the Twin Cities, the experimental design created paired communities with and without fair-employment legislation. Minneapolis had a law; St. Paul did not. Here was a chance to study the effect of governmental intervention on the employment of northern minorities. By the summer of 1949, the Minneapolis Fair Employment Practice Commission had been in operation long enough to make its effects distinguishable, yet not long enough to obliterate the *status quo ante*.

In Minnesota, the state legislature had just voted down an F.E.P.C. bill. Legislators had hurled contradictory claims and counterclaims at one another. Though offering no facts, proponents proclaimed their conviction that the Minneapolis ordinance had achieved positive results. Opponents uttered dire predictions, again without proof: "An employer's business may be injured by hiring minority group members; employees will not be willing to work with the members of minority groups, and this will cause difficulties for the employer and will injure his business."[1]

Much of the opposition to a statewide F.E.P.C. appeared to come from those least familiar with such legislation. Conversely, employers who had experienced it in operation tended to be more favorable. The executive secretary of the Minneapolis F.E.P.C. claimed that many Minneapolis employers who had opposed the city ordinance now favored a state law, whereas most of the opposition to a state law came from F.E.P.C.-less St. Paul.

In the meantime, fair employment began to be practiced on a limited

---

[1]Wilfred C. Leland, Jr., "Minnesota State Fair Employment Practices Bill: Answers to Points Raised by Opponents" (Minneapolis F.E.P.C. Office, n.d.), p. 3. (Mimeographed.)

scale in both Minneapolis and St. Paul. The largest stores in both cities were the focus of a concerted assault and subsequently placed the first Negroes in the history of those stores behind sales counters and office desks.

To these managers I went to ask about the pressures to which they had succumbed and about their experiences with the new employees themselves, the white employees, and the customers. I also interviewed the competitors of the pioneering managers—those who still resisted changing their personnel policies—to probe their expectations. And both groups of managers were asked how they felt about F.E.P.C.[2]

The Negro Community in the Twin Cities

The proportion of Negroes in Minneapolis and St. Paul had not changed much for several decades.[3]

Minneapolis' 5,800 Negroes were 1.1% of a total population of 540,000. St. Paul's 6,000 Negroes formed a larger proportion (1.8%) of a smaller total (340,000). Compared to the United States as a whole, the Twin Cities had only one-seventh the national ratio.[4]

In each city the percentage of Negroes had increased slightly over the prewar figure, presumably the result of migrants seeking new industrial

[2]The managers' views were supplemented by interviews with staff members of three major pressure groups—the two Urban Leagues and the Minneapolis Fair Employment Practices Commission. Due allowance must be made for the fact that both store managers and agency executives report and interpret events from their own perspectives.

To complete the picture, several other kinds of information would have been useful. (1) I took for granted the existence of Negroes capable of skilled work who had not been given jobs commensurate with their abilities. The St. Paul Urban League provided partial evidence, but no one knew exactly how many Twin Cities Negroes were "underemployed" nor what their experiences had been in trying to break through the barriers to retail employment. (2) For direct observation of customer behavior and polling of customer attitudes, I drew on an incomplete Minneapolis study and a more thorough one in New York. (3) No direct studies of the behavior and attitudes of white employees were available. With the exception of reports on the integration of Negro combat troops during World War II, at best a far-fetched parallel, I had to rely on the managers' reports about their employees' reactions to Negro fellow-employees. (4) Finally, the Negroes placed in skilled positions were an untapped source of information. Observation and measurement of job performance could have checked on the managers' subjective evaluations. It would have been useful to find out how the first Negro employees perceived the customer, employee, and supervisory relationships that they experienced.

[3]Estimates of the Negro and total population were provided by the Urban League and the City Planning Board, respectively, in each city.

[4]We do not know for certain the consequences of the Negro-white population ratio for social change. Presumably, the smaller the Negro population, (1) the less visible it is to employers as a source of potential employees during a labor shortage, and (2) the less bargaining power the Negro community has in terms of consumer purchasing power, political voting power, the threat of massive demonstrations, and

jobs during World War II. The prewar employment picture had been gloomy. The Governor's Interracial Commission (1945)[5] reported that in 1930 three-fourths of all Minneapolis Negro workers were in domestic service, and two-thirds of those were concentrated on the staff of three hotels. But these workers were the fortunate few. During the depression most Twin Cities Negroes were unable to find work of any kind. In 1936, 62% of all Negro families in St. Paul were on relief though only 23% of the white families were.

Three years later Gunnar Myrdal visited Minneapolis and found most Negroes still unemployed:

> The local Urban League worked hard to find employment outlets but with scant success. The white people I met were all well informed about the criminality and viciousness in the Negro slum quarters but, on the whole, totally ignorant about Negro unemployment. They had given practically no thought to the possible causal relations between economic distress and morals (Myrdal, 1944).

The wartime labor shortage was a boon to local Negroes. Twelve to fourteen hundred Negroes went to work at the Twin Cities Arsenal. After the war, the Arsenal closed, but Negroes had gained skills which paved the way to better jobs in other industries. The Minneapolis Community Self-Survey found in 1946 that 60% of the local firms employing Negroes had first hired them after Pearl Harbor.[6]

Few wartime gains were made outside of industry. Whereas the labor shortage in Chicago opened up jobs for Negroes outside the Black Belt as clerks in stores and as waitresses in restaurants and at soda fountains (Drake and Cayton, 1945), no such breaks occurred in the Twin Cities job ceiling. Only after the war did Minneapolis and St. Paul begin to catch up with the employment gains in bigger northern cities.

The Breakthrough Timetable

Before 1947 Minneapolis had been slightly more "liberal" than St. Paul, although the job ceiling was rigid in both cities. One store began employing Negro stenographers in 1939, and another boasted a Negro in the public-contact (but more service than sales) position of a shoe-repair department.

the like. John Leggett suggests:
> Where Negroes constitute from one-fifth to two-fifths of a city's population, perhaps a different model applies, one more concerned with power relations between white and Negro communities. Perhaps where there are very few Negroes living in a community, Negroes must depend largely upon the paternalism of their own middle class, plus the efforts of the white liberal community.

[5]Dates in parentheses refer to the date of publication of references listed alphabetically by author at the back of the book.

[6]"Report and Recommendations" (n.d.), p. 4. (Mimeographed.)

These were the only breakthroughs before 1946. They were isolated instances. They set in motion no trend corresponding to the repercussions of the policy change by a St. Paul store that in January 1948 hired the first full-time Negro salesgirl. The difference reflects the fact that the prewar cases involved idiosyncratic management initiative, whereas the 1948 hirings came in response to widespread pressure.

Table 1-1

Negro Employment Breakthroughs in Minneapolis and St. Paul by Job Classification and by Year

	JANITORIAL		OTHER SERVICE		SALES		CLERICAL		TOTAL	
YEAR:	Mpls.	St.P.	Mpls.	St.P.	Mpls.	St.P.	Mpls.	St.P.	Mpls.	St.P.
[before 1947]	—	—	—	—	[1]	[1]	[3]	[0]	—	—
1947	1	0	0	2	0	0	0	1	1	3
1948	0	1	6	0	5	3	0	0	11	4
1949 (8 mo.)	0	0	1	1	1	0	2	0	4	1
Total*	1	1	7	3	6	3	2	1	16	8

*Under the Minneapolis F.E.P.C. law, 16 employment breakthroughs occurred in 29 stores (55%). In St. Paul during the same years without F.E.P.C., eight breakthroughs occurred in 21 stores (38%). The critical ratio of the difference is 1.19, probability less than 0.2.

In 1946 a few stirrings occurred in the direction of fair employment—the first in almost ten years (see Table 1-1). One store hired its first Negro stenographer and subsequently added others. The first Negro office worker at another store survived only until 1948 and was not mentioned by the manager as a basis for predicting the future. The first Negro salesgirl was hired part-time in 1946 and became full-time in 1948. The year 1947 was a quiet one; most changes were restricted to blue-collar jobs except for a single girl assigned to both switchboard and office work until "the job was abolished in 1948."

The breakthrough year in both cities was 1948. The St. Paul store that two years earlier had hired a part-time Negro salesgirl shifted her to full-time and added a second girl. Despite the passage of the Minneapolis F.E.P.C. ordinance almost a full year earlier, the first break in the barrier to Negro sales employment did not occur there but in St. Paul. After this store pioneered, eight more followed suit in the next 12 months.

But the momentum did not carry over into 1949, when store managers felt the pinch of a recession and were hiring no one, white or Negro. Further progress was difficult except when a personnel manager took a personal interest in a Negro employee (the one upgraded to office work) or in the welfare of Negroes generally (the other new clerical employee). Further, despite the fact that openings occurred at four different job levels between 1947 and 1949, not a single store opened up more than one level. The 24 policy changes in Table 1-1 represent 24 different stores. Rather than being a general crumbling of job barriers, change came one notch at a time.

In a comparison of the two cities, 16 of the 29 Minneapolis stores (55%) and eight of the 21 St. Paul stores (38%) opened new categories to Negro employment. In each city, half the breakthroughs occurred in blue-collar jobs and half in white-collar jobs. The breakthroughs were concentrated in the classifications immediately above and below the blue-collar/white-collar line.

Job opportunities for St. Paul Negroes expanded only two-thirds as fast as for Minneapolis Negroes after the F.E.P.C. began in Minneapolis. Later we shall see that basic changes in both cities can be credited to primarily the Urban Leagues and managerial liberalism. The margin favoring Minneapolis reflects a larger number of pressure groups there, including the F.E.P.C. and the Joint Committee for Employment Opportunity. While less prominent than the Urban League in securing change, these agencies gave added impetus to the Minneapolis movement toward fair-employment practices. The Minneapolis F.E.P.C. ordinance helped open new job classifications to Negroes, although it was only one of several forces conspiring together.

Comparing the Negro and total employment figures for 17 Minneapolis stores over the same 1947–1949 interval shows how much the total number of Negro employees increased after the F.E.P.C. was enacted.

Table 1-2

Changes in Number of Negro Employees and Total Employees in 17 Minneapolis Stores between 1947 and 1949

| NUMBER OF NEGRO EMPLOYEES | | | TOTAL EMPLOYEES | NUMBER OF NEGROES |
MAY 1947	AUGUST 1949	NET GAIN	NET GAIN	IN NEW JOB CATEGORIES
0	12	12	0	4 Salesgirls
7	15	8	0	1 Salesgirl
1	6	5	—75	1 Other service
5	7	2	0	
3	5	2	45	1 Clerical
6	7	1	10	2 Clerical
2	3	1	—1	1 Other service
5	5	0	0	
2	2	0	—5	
2	2	0	—3	
1	1	0	—6	
1	1	0	53	
0	0	0	25	
4	3	—1	19	
10	8	—2	0	
7	5	—2	200	
3	1	—2	10	
				+8 above ceiling
Total 59	83	+24	+272	+2 below ceiling

Source:

The 1947 figures are from a study by Felice Wender, which is in the files of the Minneapolis Urban League. She studied 17 stores employing 70% of the total employees in my entire sample of 29 Minneapolis stores. The stores are arranged in the table in order of magnitude of change in the number of Negro employees from greatest gain to greatest loss.

Table 1-2 shows that Negro mobility occurred exclusively in stores where the total number of Negro employees increased. Where the number remained constant or became smaller, no upgrading of individual employees into new classifications occurred. Where Negroes were added at higher levels, new jobs generally came in addition to, rather than at the expense of, old ones.

The net change for Negroes in 27 months was a gain of 24 jobs. The two largest stores account for most of this increase (20 of the 24). With the exception of these two stores (which were the only ones adding sales-girls), gains and losses were fairly evenly balanced. There is no correlation between changes in total staff and changes in the number of Negro employees; thus, changes in Negro employment were neither proportional to nor even necessarily in the same direction as trends in total staff.

Negroes gained jobs faster than whites during this period. Whereas white employees increased by only 3.5% over 1947, Negro employees increased by 41%. The net gain of 24 Negro jobs was not randomly distributed. Ten were added in positions higher than Negroes had ever gone before in those particular stores, and eight of these were placed above the previously impenetrable, community-wide job ceiling. For almost 9% of the net increase in retail jobs during this period to go to Negroes (when they were hardly more than 1% of the local population), and for almost half of this increase to involve barrier-breaking upward mobility emphasizes the importance of 1947–49 in the history of Negro employment in Minneapolis.

Chapter 2

Negro Employment: Segregation and Tokenism

Compared to the prewar period, the 1940s may have been a decade of spectacular breakthroughs in the North. Yet the baseline was so low that even relatively great strides left northern Negroes pitifully underemployed. In the Twin Cities the postwar breakthroughs superimposed a thin veneer of token employment on the old hulk of segregation.

More than four-fifths of the Twin Cities stores employed some Negroes in 1949, and 90% of the stores had employed Negroes either then or in the past. Three managers recalled that Negroes had applied for jobs but had never been hired. Only two stores had never had any direct contact with Negroes as past, present, or potential employees.

Table 2-1
Stores Ever Employing Negroes or Ever Receiving Negro Applications, by City

	MINNEAPOLIS	ST. PAUL
Employed Negroes in August 1949	80%	86%
Employed Negroes in past only	7	10
Received Negro applications but never hired any	10	0
Never received any Negro applications	3	4
Total	100%	100%
Number of stores	29	21

Since Minneapolis had an F.E.P.C. and St. Paul did not, I expected Negroes to be more widely employed there. Table 2-1 shows that this was not the case. Indeed, active discrimination (in the form of consistently rejecting all Negroes who applied) was admitted by only Minneapolis managers. Obviously, passing a fair-employment ordinance did not make employment immediately fair.

However, if we make allowance for the smaller proportion of Negroes in the Minneapolis population and the more specialized stores in the Minneapolis sample (see Appendix), we should conclude that the two cities were essentially similar in the pervasiveness of Negro employment. The small Negro minority was distributed remarkably widely among the 50 stores.

This distribution is one result of the job ceiling. The ceiling is that point in the occupational hierarchy above which the qualifications of Negro applicants are not examined. Negroes are automatically disqualified, regardless of skill, solely on the ground of color.

The Industry and Labor Committee of the Minneapolis Self-Survey reported, however, that Negroes were distributed less extensively among the *total* retail business of the city. Fully 60% of the wholesale and retail businesses of the city employed no Negroes, Jews, or Japanese-Americans.[1] This lower total distribution of minority members reflects the smaller size of businesses excluded from my study. The Self-Survey found that "the average-size firm in Minneapolis is small (28 employees); that of firms not employing the minorities is even smaller (20 employees); while those employing minorities are concentrated among the larger-than-average-size establishments (55 employees)."[2] In my study, the median labor force for stores not employing Negroes was 70, compared to a median of 150 for stores with Negro employees. In addition, in 1949 Negroes were rarely employed outside the downtown area. Three of the four large suburban stores in my survey employed no Negroes at all.

The Minneapolis Self-Survey also found that 48% of the companies who employed Negroes at all limited them to unskilled jobs. This situation long prevailed throughout the United States. Despite the fact that wholesale and retail trade was listed by Charles Johnson (1943) as one of "38 general industrial or service groups in which at least half of the Negro workers were employed in capacities above the unskilled labor category," he recognized that the retail job ceiling was very low. He pointed out that jobs "in which there is contact with the public in the capacity of salesmen or skilled operatives, such as clerks in stores ... " were among those in which "Negro numbers are most strictly limited." More specifically, Myrdal (1944) cited the 1930 census figure for Negroes as 0.7% of all "female clerks and kindred workers" (whereas Negroes are 10% of the American population). In another northern city, where Negroes constituted 7% of the population, the situation was the same:

> In 1930 almost 100,000 people in Chicago were involved in "selling" and nearly 60,000 were serving the needs of commerce and industry with note-book and typewriter. Negroes were employed in these capacities in a proportion of less than one in a hundred! Wherever Negro members of this small group were found, if they were not in government positions, they were usually working in Negro neighborhoods (Drake and Cayton, 1945).

[1] No breakdown is given for stores having Jews and/or Japanese but no Negroes, a presumably higher figure.

[2] "Report and Recommendations," p. 4. The 40% of all firms that did employ minority-group members embraced 80% of the total labor force of the city.

The Negro Worker in Minnesota reported that there were only "about 80" small Negro businesses in the entire state of Minnesota. Hence the Twin Cities offered few white-collar jobs to Negroes as employees of Negro businessmen.[3]

The situation in the Twin Cities was no different from that in Chicago. Table 2-2 portrays the distribution by job classification of Negro employment in 1949 and in the past, together with applications for jobs.

Table 2-2
Stores Ever Employing Negroes or Ever Receiving Negro Applications, by Job Classification and by City

	MINNEAPOLIS	ST. PAUL
JANITORIAL		
Employed Negroes in August 1949	70%	71%
Employed Negroes in past only	3	15
Received Negro applications but never hired any	10	5
Never received any Negro applications	17	9
Total	100%	100%
OTHER SERVICES		
Employed Negroes in August 1949	52%	71%
Employed Negroes in past only	21	10
Received Negro applications but never hired any	7	5
Never received any Negro applications	20	14
Total	100%	100%
SALES		
Employed Negroes in August 1949	17%	19%
Employed Negroes in past only	7	0
Received Negro applications but never hired any	21	29
Never received any Negro applications	55	52
Total	100%	100%
CLERICAL		
Employed Negroes in August 1949	14%	0%
Employed Negroes in past only	3	5
Received Negro applications but never hired any	21	33
Never received any Negro applications	62	62
Total	100%	100%
MANAGERIAL		
Never received any Negro applications	100%	100%
Number of stores	29	21

Negroes were employed about equally in Minneapolis and St. Paul as janitors, salesgirls, and managers (the latter being zero in each city). In the "other service" category, substantially more St. Paul stores employed Negroes. Conversely, there were no Negro clerical workers in any St. Paul stores, whereas 14% of the Minneapolis stores had at least one each.

The tendency of more St. Paul stores to employ Negroes below the job ceiling, and of fewer to employ them above the ceiling, is presented

[3]The industrial secretary of the Minneapolis Urban League reported in July 1950 that there were no Negro-owned retail stores in Minneapolis.

graphically in Figure 2-A, which presents the combined total of stores employing Negroes at each job level either in 1949 or previously. The St. Paul pattern slopes off more steeply, starting higher and ending lower than that for Minneapolis.

Figure 2-A

Percentage of Stores Ever Employing Negroes, by Job Classification, for Minneapolis and St. Paul, 1949

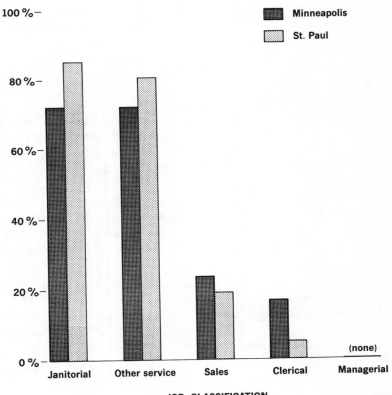

If the Negro population of the Twin Cities had been randomly distributed in employment throughout the job classifications, the population would have been employed equally often at each job level. The fact that Negroes were not employed equally often at each job level reflects the job ceiling.[4] The

---

[4] Presumably that fact also reflects lower educational qualifications and the other employment handicaps associated with being Negro in twentieth-century America. Many of these handicaps stem from the past operation of the job ceiling in a

more frequently stores employ Negroes below the ceiling (as in St. Paul), and the less they employ Negroes above the ceiling, the more rigid the ceiling is in that community. Since the slope for Minneapolis in Figure 2-A is more nearly horizontal, Minneapolis had departed further from the traditional restriction of Negroes to service jobs. This observation confirms one of our expectations, that more Minneapolis firms would employ Negroes in skilled and public-contact jobs, whereas more St. Paul firms would employ Negroes in unskilled or semiskilled work. However, this does not prove that the difference was due to the Minneapolis F.E.P.C. law. (We shall see later that the managers viewed the F.E.P.C. as only one of several factors responsible.)

The distribution of Negroes at various job levels reveals clearly where the Twin Cities job ceiling was located. More than three-quarters of the 50 stores employed Negroes as janitors and in other-service capacities. By contrast, the incidence for sales, clerical, and managerial work was 22%, 12%, and 0%. The sharp drop from "other service" to sales locates the ceiling.[5]

The term "ceiling" deserves elaboration. The word implies the stratification of jobs into high and low statuses. Generally, the jobs that involve the greatest physical exertion, the dirtiest work, the least skill, and no responsibility are esteemed least and lowest paid. Conversely, white-collar jobs requiring skill and responsibility usually provide greater income and prestige.

In white society every man is supposed to get the job for which he is qualified.[6] "Ability counts," as the slogan goes. There is no ceiling, we say, for the man with talent. We hail the bank president who began as office boy. One St. Paul stock boy will never reach the top. Trained as an accountant, he would make a capable store executive in the estimation of his employer. But he is stuck in the stock room because he is a Negro, and Negroes are held down by the job ceiling.

At certain times in the past, and in certain parts of the country, this dividing line acted not only as a ceiling for Negroes but also as a floor for whites. Jobs below the ceiling were "Negro jobs," which whites would not lower themselves to fill. The depression broke up many of these Negro monopolies. Although there are a few "Negro jobs" in the Twin Cities retail field, the ceiling bars Negro employment above the ceiling more than white employment below it.

vicious cycle of underemployment-produced despair conveyed to children who in turn drop out of school and are then poorly equipped for skilled employment.

[5]Later I suggest why the addition of a few employees above the service level does not mean that the location of the ceiling has been changed.

[6]This is especially true for white Anglo-Saxon Protestants. Negroes are only one of many groups that suffer from employment handicaps. Few groups, however, encounter as rigid barriers as Negroes do.

As we saw previously, the Minneapolis Self-Survey found that half of the companies employing Negroes confined them to unskilled labor. If janitors, porters, and maids are the unskilled workers in retail stores, we have a basis for comparison. One-sixth of our St. Paul stores and almost a third of our Minneapolis stores employing any Negroes hired them for unskilled labor exclusively. Both of these proportions are smaller than the 48% for Minneapolis businesses generally. Closer up, the retail record looks still better, since six of the ten stores with "Negro jobs" had only one Negro employee—the janitor. The great majority of stores employing Negroes placed them at least in the slightly skilled "other service" category as well as in janitorial work.

Negro applications for jobs complement Negro employment patterns. Below the job ceiling, more Negroes applied for jobs at stores failing to hire them in Minneapolis than in St. Paul. Above the job ceiling, the St. Paul stores without skilled Negro employees more often received applications. Since fewer nonhiring Minneapolis stores had Negroes apply for skilled jobs, the presumed encouragement of pioneering applications by the F.E.P.C. law failed to materialize.

Another effect of the wide St. Paul distribution of Negro applications for high-status jobs is to neutralize the flexibility in the Minneapolis job ceiling. The proportion of employers in active contact with Negroes above the ceiling (combining present and past employment with applications) is identical for the two cities for both sales and clerical work: 48% of the stores in each city have had Negro salesgirls or applicants, and 38% in each have had contact with Negroes about clerical work.[7]

The proportion of Negroes employed was more than their ratio in the total population. In Minneapolis 1.6 times as many Negroes were employed proportionate to the population, and St. Paul had 1.3 times as many. This difference suggests that the Minneapolis F.E.P.C. ordinance and other local factors had at best only slightly enlarged the number of retail job openings for Negroes. For the Twin Cities combined, 50% more Negroes were employed in the large stores than would be expected on the basis of population. But since most of the stores excluded from this study hired no Negroes, this did not mean that Negroes were flooding the field of retail trade.

The proportions of Negroes employed at various job levels are shown in Table 2-3.

The absolute percentage of Negroes among the total employees at the three lowest job levels was larger in St. Paul than in Minneapolis. However, when allowance is made for the larger proportion of Negroes in the St. Paul population, approximately one-third more Negroes were employed in

---

[7]If the sales clerk that a Minneapolis nonrespondent is known to have employed is included.

Table 2-3

Proportion of Negro Employees by Job Classification and by City

JOB CLASSIFICATION	NEGROES AS PERCENTAGE OF TOTAL EMPLOYEES	
	MINNEAPOLIS	ST. PAUL
Janitorial	29.1%	33.6%
Other service	4.5%	5.0%
Sales	0.2%	0.2%
Clerical	0.3%	0.0%
Managerial	0.0%	0.0%
Total	1.8%	2.4%
Total number of employees	11,734	5.829

Minneapolis than in St. Paul at these same three levels. This consistently greater proportion of Minneapolis Negro employees, which carries over even more conspicuously into the clerical level, would demonstrate the value of F.E.P.C. provided it could be shown that the difference, especially above the job ceiling, was the result of the Minneapolis F.E.P.C. law. Since that cannot be shown (see Part 2 on the dynamics of how the job ceiling has been pierced), it cannot be said that the statistics in Table 2-3 confirm my hypothesis.

The job ceiling is reflected even more strongly in Table 2-3 than in Table 2-2. In the latter, the ratio between the percentage of stores employing Negroes as janitors and the percentage employing them as office workers is less than 10 to 1 (70% and 8% respectively). But Table 2-3 indicates that the *number* of Negro janitors *employed* was 30.9% of the total cleaning force of the 50 stores, whereas eight Negro office workers were only 0.2% of the total office staff, a ratio of more than 100 to 1. The job ceiling not only limits the number of stores employing Negroes at higher levels but even more effectively limits the number of Negroes employed.

Negroes on the sales forces of the Twin Cities department stores were one-sixth of what they would have been if Negroes were first-class citizens in employment.[8] The discrepancy was even larger in New York City, where "although 8% of the New York City population is colored, only four-tenths of 1% of the department-store sales force are Negroes" (Saenger, 1948). Therefore, in New York department stores only one-twentieth as many

---

[8]Such a comparison assumes a utopian state of affairs in which Negroes had risen to full educational, social, and economic equality with whites and had free access to jobs in all fields. In 1949 none of these conditions was true. Hence employment proportionate to the population was a long-range goal that could not be achieved immediately because of the smaller proportion of Negroes with the requisite skills and sophistication for sales or clerical work.

With Negroes now at an intermediate stage in the trend toward fair employment, Professor Theodore Caplow predicts that they will be "excessively" employed in skilled retail jobs. "Sales and stenographic work are the only jobs with adequate public school training facilities. Training for most other occupations costs money, so economically impoverished Negroes are likely to concentrate here. Furthermore, retail employment is relatively fluid, which fits the greater mobility of the Negro population."

Negro sales persons were employed as would be expected from their presence in the population.

Of more than 9,000 sales clerks in the Twin Cities in 1949, 17 were Negroes: 16 girls and one man (our borderline case, in charge of a shoe-repair department). Negro salesgirls were employed first in the largest stores, chiefly department stores. Moreover, the largest stores tended to employ a few more Negroes than smaller stores did. Hence there was a rough parallel between the size of the total sales force and the size of the Negro sales force. Nevertheless, despite the claim of some managers that a quota formula was used in hiring Negroes, not a single store in either city had yet filled its quota of salesgirls.

The job ceiling not only depressed the number of Negro sales clerks substantially below the quota but also assigned Negroes to a disproportionate number of the less desirable jobs. Figure 2-B illustrates the striking contrast between the Negro job pyramid and the total job pyramid in the Twin Cities.[9]

It is clear from the total job pyramid that retail stores are characteristically sales enterprises. The 52% of all employees engaged in selling was serviced by 21% doing manual labor on goods and buildings and by 27% performing the bookkeeping and managerial functions.

Janitorial work, least important numerically in the total picture, is the modal category for Twin Cities Negroes, with other semiskilled manual labor a close second. A few years before, these were the only jobs Negroes held. By 1949, however, 2% of the Negroes employed by the retail stores had clerical jobs, and 5% were engaged in selling, while the remaining 93% were still below the ceiling.

The concentration of Negroes below the ceiling produces complete occupational segregation in some stores. Janitorial work is especially often a "Negro job." Of five small stores hiring only one janitor apiece, three chose Negroes. More significantly, eight of 45 stores with janitorial staffs of two or more hired only Negroes. That this practice was often intentional can be seen from the large number of Negroes (82) employed on segregated janitorial staffs. Two stores had all-Negro janitorial staffs of 20 each, and a third had 28.

In addition, Negroes performed all the "other supporting services" in three small stores. All three also had only Negroes as janitors. None of the 11 stores employing Negroes on a segregated basis for janitorial and other-service work had ever employed a Negro above the job ceiling.[10] Segre-

[9]Note that, if the comparison were with the white, rather than the total, job distribution, the janitorial base of the upper pyramid would be a third narrower.

[10]With the semi-exception of a chain with three Negro fountain girls concentrated in one of their many local stores.

Figure 2-B

**Total Job Pyramid and Negro Employment Pyramid in 50
Twin Cities Stores, 1949***

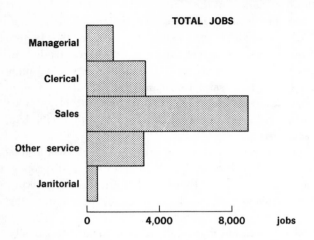

TOTAL JOBS

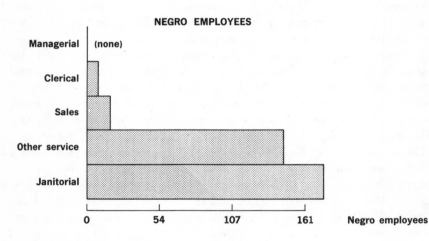

NEGRO EMPLOYEES

Source: Table 2-3
* (Scaled to ratio of total population to Negro population, or
74.5 to 1.)

gation thus cut both ways; whenever low-status jobs were reserved for
Negroes, the good jobs were correspondingly saved for whites.[11]

Skilled Negro workers were highly concentrated in department stores.
Half the department stores had at least one salesgirl apiece, and one had

[11]It should be remembered, however, that five stores with all-Negro janitorial
staffs had mixed employment at the "other service" level and that the 11 segregationist managers were hardly more than one-fifth of the total number of managers.

an office worker as well. Negro applications for high-status jobs in stores where Negroes were not yet employed were concentrated in this same type of store. Only drug stores, one of which had Negro salesgirls (at the fountain) and all of which had Negro applicants for sales and clerical jobs, approximated department stores in providing avenues for, or pressure toward, upward occupational mobility.

No other types of store employed a single sales person, although at least one variety store had done so in the past. In view of the similarity between merchandise sold by variety stores and by those counters of department stores at which Negroes have usually been placed (bargain basements, housewares, and so on), it seems surprising that variety stores received so few Negro applications for sales positions. The median St. Paul department store numbered 763 employees, whereas the median variety store had only one-tenth as many. Thus smaller size may attract fewer applications.

The remaining types of stores—clothing, furniture, and hardware—exhibit consciousness of kind; they think of their own groups as special cases. When the personnel managers of those stores are asked to evaluate the experience of the department stores in the employment of Negro salesgirls, the characteristic response is "It's been O.K., I guess, but it doesn't apply to us." High standards of knowledge and experience for the sales personnel of department stores are often cited, but in 1949 there was no chance in the Twin Cities for a Negro to gain the qualifying sales experience even if he had the proper knowledge.

Theodore Caplow has suggested that specialized stores depend as much on the prestige value of the store's atmosphere and name as on quality of merchandise to attract customers. A carefully cultivated relationship between salesman and customer provides middle-class customers who have social aspirations with the feeling that trading at such a store raises their status. This skillfully nurtured psychological impression would be jeopardized by the hiring of Negro sales clerks, given the quasi-professional relationship between clerk and customer.

The consciousness of kind exhibited by each type of store springs from the dynamics of the retail economy. Stores compete with others of their own kind. A hardware store competes with other hardware stores and is influenced by what they do, if it is influenced at all. Even though a department store may have a hardware department, that department is submerged in the whole complex, so that neither the department-store manager nor the hardware-store manager thinks of the other as a competitor.

Consciousness of kind limits the potential chain reaction in hiring Negro sales persons. Imitative hiring, which is motivated by both recognition of successful Negro accomplishment and competitive pressure for Negro customers, occurs almost exclusively *within* a group of stores. Once the job ceiling was pierced by the first Negro salesgirl in a department store, other department stores in both cities followed suit. Consciousness of kind has complementary functions: (a) slowing the spread of new personnel policies from category to category but (b) facilitating contagious innovation once a group is successfully infected. Hence, getting Negro salesgirls into department stores provided little basis for predicting their employment elsewhere. Efforts to get Negro salesgirls hired in other types of stores might be most appropriately directed toward one group of stores at a time and focused on the most cooperative store within that group.

Ten stores with no Negro employees whatsoever were widely scattered among the various types of stores. Similarly, the four Minneapolis stores employing Negro office workers represent four different types of stores, a dispersion strikingly different from the concentration of salesgirls in a single type.

That women's clothing, men's clothing, and furniture stores in addition to one large department store had Negro clerical workers can be easily understood. There had been little pressure to date for employment of Negroes in clerical positions. In each of the pioneering stores, someone in top management took the initiative. One manager had been a director of the Urban League for many years, and the other three had humanitarian motives. That three specialized stores chose to hire clerical rather than sales workers is also understandable. Customer reaction does not have to be faced when a Negro girl is assigned to a mailing machine or a typewriter. And white office employees are more easily controllable in a specialized store, where clerical workers are so few (respectively 20, 20, and 10) that the boss's personal views can be influential.

Stores can be classified not only by type of merchandise but by strength of competitive position as well. There are two ideal types. One of these may be labeled "patriarchal." Its distinguishing characteristics include (1) local ownership and management concentrated in one or a few hands; (2) corporate longevity with corresponding emphasis on the store's prestige and name; and (3) high-class status of store and customers. These characteristics produce an unusually stable labor force and a degree of customer loyalty that place the store in a strong competitive position. The opposite extreme is a chain store (owned in Chicago or New York) that has recently opened its Twin Cities' branch, whose management and customers are middle class, and that has high mobility in management and employees. Pressed from above by the far-away owners' interest in monetary profits and pressed locally by keen rivalry for unattached middle-class customers, chain stores operate on precarious, competitive margins.

This typology helps to explain the location of the few clerical workers. All three specialized stores hiring Negro clerical workers were patriarchal. All were locally owned and had been in operation an average of 43 years. The two clothing stores were notably aristocratic in clientele. Under such circumstances, the personal views of the head of the store are persuasive. Where those views were sympathetic to the employment of Negroes, the store operators could afford to take whatever risk might be involved in experimenting with Negro office workers. In other patriarchal stores, views unsympathetic to Negroes were sometimes encountered, and under such circumstances, no Negro clerical workers were hired. By contrast, some managers of chain-type stores were personally sympathetic to the employment of Negroes above the ceiling but felt that their own weak competitive situation and the remote ownership did not allow them to risk anything new. The store situation thus controls the extent to which store managers feel free to follow their personal desires in employment policies.

Tokens and Quotas

By August 1949, the campaign to place more Negroes in skilled retail jobs had bogged down in the Twin Cities. That employers were feeling the pinch of a recession and were wary about hiring anyone is part of the explanation. But the wave of department-store hirings of Negro salesgirls had also exhausted itself. Other types of stores were not yet convinced that integration was a safe venture. And the department stores themselves showed little inclination to take on more Negroes at skilled levels.

Urban League officials were beginning to wonder how much they had really accomplished:

> There isn't a store yet in [this city] where a qualified Negro girl can walk in and be sure of getting a sales job for which a vacancy exists. The Urban League always has to intervene. It's all token employment so far. In the better jobs, characteristically, one Negro is hired, the employer is satisfied with the job done, but then no more are hired. It's a hard fight for us, one notch at a time. Breaking the ice is the worst hurdle, however. Every placement above the former ceiling makes subsequent ones easier (personal comment to author).

Tokenism is the employment of one Negro per job category as a representative of his race. The employer's motive is to put up a good front to Negro and liberal white publics and to appease pressure groups. Under these conditions, placing a second Negro in a similar position at the same store can be almost as difficult as placing the first. The job ceiling was not raised from one level to another in the occupational hierarchy. Instead, isolated Negroes were hired on an exceptional basis.

In large stores employing more than 100 persons, the token concept is often converted into a quota system for minority groups. I did not ask directly about employment quotas, but three respondents spontaneously mentioned the idea. A St. Paul manager with 150 employees applied the quota concept to his store as a whole:

We have always had a few Negroes and they have always been satisfactory. We purposely hire some in order to be representative—we try to hire all groups. We have no prejudice of any kind for or against any group. Our two Negroes [both janitors] out of 150 employees is equal to the proportion of Negroes in the St. Paul population and shows we are doing our share.

As far as *number* of jobs is concerned, his quota was full. But the problem facing Twin Cities Negroes was not so much a lack of retail jobs, or unemployment, as the wrong kind of jobs, or underemployment. Ten Twin Cities stores filled their quota by hiring Negro janitors. The Urban Leagues were justifiably skeptical when "doing our share" is confined to traditional dirty work. Under such circumstances, a filled quota acts as a barrier against employing Negroes at higher levels.

In the largest stores the quota concept is sometimes applied to a particular category of jobs, such as the sales staff. This practice was implied by another personnel manager: "I would never feel the company could use too many Negro salesgirls but it could probably use one or two." The quota concept lies behind the previously cited admission by a department-store executive that the number of Negro salesgirls is held to the level set by his competitors.

Wherever a store has less than its "proportionate" share of Negroes, the quota concept may be used as a lever to secure more jobs. This potentiality existed in one large store that espoused a quota philosophy but failed to carry it out in practice. Asked how many Negro employees the store had, the personnel manager said he did not know but was pretty sure the company tried to hire Negroes in proportion to the local population. When I suggested that this would mean several dozen Negroes, the manager visibly jumped and admitted he was sure there were not that many. When a subordinate later reported that the correct figure was 12, the personnel manager shook his head and confessed, "That is less than I thought we had."

In large stores and in the retail field as a whole, the quota concept is a useful analytical tool that may be applied as a standard for evaluating the actual number of Negroes employed at particular job levels. Figure 2-B illustrates the contrasting shapes of the Negro and the total retail job pyramids in the Twin Cities. The quota provides another way of comparing these pyramids drawn to proportionate scales by superimposing the total job pyramid on the Negro distribution.

Figure 2-C portrays the discrepancies between actual Negro employment and the quotas corresponding to the total retail jobs in my sample of 50 stores. If I had covered all the stores in the Twin Cities, the quotas would have been larger, but the number of Negro employees would not have increased proportionately since smaller stores seldom employ Negroes even below the ceiling.

Figure 2-C

Quota Surpluses and Deficiencies by Job Classification

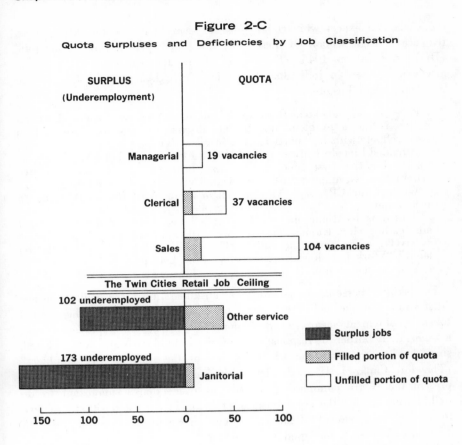

Source: Table 2-3

Figure 2-C shows a heavy excess of Negroes employed below the job ceiling. The 275 Negroes employed there in excess of the quota exceed the deficiency of 160 unfilled jobs above the ceiling for these stores. However, the total quota for all stores in the Twin Cities (based on the 1948 occupational census figure of 71,000 persons engaged in retail trade) was 950. Since less than half this figure (352) was on the payroll of the 50 biggest stores, it seems unlikely that retail business *as a whole* had been overly generous with jobs for Negroes. Even for those who do get jobs, the ceiling gives a large proportion of undesirable jobs to Negroes and bars them from skilled positions with higher wages, more prestige, and more challenging work.

That skewed job distributions in northern cities were not entirely the result of a lack of trained Negroes is suggested by Chicago figures from the same era: "Of every ten teen-age white girls, nine are in high school. Of these, six can expect white-collar jobs. Of every ten teen-age Negro girls, five are in high school. Of these, only one can expect a white-collar job" (Drake and Cayton, 1945). The impact of this denial of economic opportunity can be seen in individual terms in a case history published by the St. Paul Urban League:

> Mr. ————, age 32. Born in Brainerd, Minnesota, where discrimination is not a problem, due to the absence of Negroes. Educated in local schools with free participation in all activities.
>
> Attended Lincoln University and Howard University, both Negro schools where, for the first time, he became aware of the problem of discrimination. Graduated from American University of Accounting.
>
> Worked for CPA and Navy Department in Washington, D.C., as an accountant.
>
> Returning to Minnesota, which he calls home, he noted numerous want ads calling for trained accountants. All applications rejected, some evasively, some sympathetically. "The job is filled." "We'll call you later." "Work has slowed up, we don't need help now."
>
> Yes, he has a job. He is now a stockboy.

For skilled persons forced to take unskilled jobs, the ceiling means frustration. For the lucky ones given breakthrough jobs above the ceiling, token employment means extra responsibility: "Token employment puts a tremendous burden of responsibility on the individual Negro who is hired, since he has to carry the whole burden of the race on his shoulders" (Theodore Caplow). If a salesgirl is hired not as an individual but to represent the Negro community, it becomes tremendously important to do well. Paradoxically, the consciousness of being in such a position can lead to a paralyzing fear of offending the customer and thus prevent the self-assurance necessary for good salesmanship.

In 1949 Twin Cities Negroes were caught between the token as a floor and the quota as a ceiling for employment in large stores above the traditional level. In small stores, the token and quota concepts yield only fractional parts of a Negro per store, so these carefully calculated approaches limited the number of stores employing Negroes. Only when these cautious mental devices are replaced by a random distribution of Negroes throughout the retail hierarchies as the result of hiring on individual merit regardless of race will the total number of Negroes employed at skilled levels measure up to the city-wide quotas that we have employed as an analytical tool. There was little evidence in 1949 that randomness was nearing.

Chapter 3

Negroes in New Jobs

How well could Negro girls perform work they had never tried before? Could novices persuade customers to buy? Could inexperienced office girls work neatly and accurately? These questions can be answered by comparing the actual experiences of the breakthrough employers in the Twin Cities with their prior expectations and with the predictions made by colleagues who had yet to hire their first Negro white-collar employees.

Negro Salesgirls

Personnel managers are responsible for both finding the right person to do each job and helping her perform well. When an employment breakthrough occurs, the manager gives special attention to the pioneer and thereby hopes to enhance her chances of success. The Twin Cities managers who employed the first Negro salesgirls took the following special precautions: (1) careful screening, (2) special training, (3) careful assignment, and (4) special supervision.

Selection

The Twin Cities Urban Leagues did the preliminary screening of Negroes who were to break through the job ceiling. The League screened applicants in its own offices before sending the best ones to managers opening up new positions. Managers generally welcomed this preselection of candidates. In a nationwide study, industrial managers similarly expressed appreciation for preselection by such agencies:

> The employers who used various special recruiting sources found that course extremely helpful for getting prescreened candidates and thus reducing the number of unqualified applicants to be interviewed (Norgren and others, 1959).

Even so, one Twin Cities manager interviewed 15 or 20 League-screened candidates before finding one he was willing to risk hiring.[1] Another

---

[1] Intensity of screening tends to diminish with successive Negroes employed by a company at a given job: "While many of the managements had adopted special prac-

selected his first Negro salesgirl because she was "an exceptional person, regardless of color." Not infrequently, a manager preferred upgrading a stock girl with whom he was already familiar to risking an unknown outsider, no matter how carefully screened and interviewed. One manager promoted from stock to sales a Negro girl who had proven her superior "personality, aggressiveness, and ambition."

Occasionally managers made mistakes in hiring new girls. One described a present Negro employee in a public contact, but nonsales, position as "just plain lazy." However, he did not generalize to all Negroes: "It's not due to her race, it's just her individual handicap; it was *our* mistake that we hired her in the first place."

Training

The largest Minneapolis store trained its first Negro salesgirls two or three times as long as usual. This measure was deemed necessary to prepare them for dealing with the expected antagonistic reactions of customers. Whereas many white employees have had sales experience elsewhere, experience is impossible for Negroes entering new job categories. Therefore, stores must choose between training otherwise qualified Negro applicants and not hiring Negroes at all.

Placement

Most personnel managers felt it was important to choose carefully the departments to which Negro salesgirls would be assigned. This decision was rarely based on the qualifications or interests of the individual employee. Rather, certain assignments were considered easier starting points for novices.

One manager described the ideal assignment as one "where the least initiative and salesmanship are required in view of low prices and a high volume of sales." Negroes assigned to kitchenwares, notions, and pet-supply counters were felt to be in situations where any clerk would be bound to succeed.

An exceptional manager found that customer-oriented placement considerations interfered with good personnel practice. A Negro girl assigned to the comparatively routine position of "transfer desk" did an adequate job there, but the manager came to realize that a sales position would have been more challenging to her, for she was a Phi Beta Kappa college graduate.

At least one manager encountered difficulty by failing to specify to a Negro employee that her job would involve occasional stock work as well as the expected salesmanship. This girl, a former actress, refused to do the stock work because she considered it to be menial. The manager was

tices in recruiting and selecting Negroes at the outset, they generally abandoned special practices after initial placements" (Norgren and others, 1959).

unable to convince her that combined sales and stock work is commonly expected in his store, regardless of an employee's race. He decided to avoid oversensitive misinterpretations in the future by placing his next prospective Negro salesgirl in stock work first and then promoting her.

Supervision

The above incident suggests that problems between employee and supervisor can affect work performance. The same actress quit when her fellow salesgirls suggested that she needed to take more baths. In view of the stereotype about Negro uncleanliness, it is not surprising that this girl interpreted the suggestion as a manifestation of prejudice. Stouffer (1949) found that in World War II Negroes often defined situations in racial terms:

> Many complaints common to soldiers of both races acquired a special significance among Negro soldiers by being invested with the quality of racial discrimination. Thus it became not merely a matter of lack of recreation facilities, poor food, slowness of promotions, and so on— all such specific points of dissatisfaction took on the potentiality of being regarded as instances of discrimination against Negroes.

Managers used such terms as "touchiness" and "sensitivity" to describe this tendency to interpret criticism as discrimination. Some managers view sensitivity over race as a major drawback to the employment of Negroes. Negroes living in our society learn by experience that discriminatory behavior can be anticipated from whites. Generalizing from previous experience, Negroes see discrimination where it may not exist. As a result, anything that looks discriminatory is liable to be magnified out of proportion. (In response to the question, "If you could talk with the President, what are the three most important questions you would want to ask him about the war and your part in it?," half of all Negro soldiers in World War II mentioned racial discrimination, whereas less than 1% of the white soldiers mentioned it (Stouffer, 1949).

Afraid of possible sensitivity, the former actress' manager decided the "baths" complaint of his white employees was potentially too explosive to handle himself. Hoping the girl would be less sensitive to a suggestion from her fellows, the manager returned the responsibility for telling her to the complainants. He might have been wiser to neutralize the racial factor by channeling criticism through other Negroes. Another possibility would have been to use the Urban League, which helps store managers with disciplinary problems. A manager may call in the League's industrial secretary, explain the facts, and leave it up to him to work out an adjustment satisfactory to both parties.[2] Not all disciplinary action requires such a

[2] For example, the Minneapolis Urban League aided a local factory in reducing absenteeism among Negro workers.

roundabout procedure, but whenever complaints coincide with stereotypes of Negro inferiority, the racial factor is best avoided by using a Negro troubleshooter.

Another store sought to avoid touchiness by a different, but equally unsatisfactory, approach. "We wanted to be friendly to this employee and went out of our way to be so by being careful to give her no reprimands. But she just stood at her counter and did nothing." Finally, white employees objected so strenuously about the favored treatment of the Negro girl that the personnel office abruptly fired her. "Special supervision" need not mean "no supervision" for new employees who require encouragement in an unfamiliar situation.

A third store minimized this problem by a different tactic: "We make it very clear to Negro employees in advance that they are on the same competitive basis as anyone else, that they must meet the usual specific quota of sales or will be fired." This manager attempted to define the job situation in purely competitive terms instead of in the Negro's usual racial perspective.

Against this background of managerial strategies for insuring sales success, we may examine the expected and the actual success of the first Negro salesgirls.

Table 3-1

Inexperienced and Experienced Managers' Estimates of Negro Sales Performance

	TYPE OF ESTIMATE	
SALES PERFORMANCE	PREDICTIONS BY INEXPERIENCED MANAGERS	EVALUATIONS BY EXPERIENCED MANAGERS
Very satisfactory	5%	23%
Satisfactory	42	31
Mixed	20	23
Unsatisfactory	30	0
Very unsatisfactory	0	15
Don't know	3	8
Total	100%	100%
Number of estimates*	40	13

Critical ratio = 44, probability > .60 for the two satisfactory categories combined.

*One manager reported both his actual experience with Negro waitresses and his prediction for Negro sales clerks as such. Two stores were rechecked and are represented by responses of two managers each.

Contrary to my expectation that inexperienced managers would be prejudiced against Negro sales ability, Table 3-1 shows considerable confidence in the potential success of presumably well-screened, trained, placed, and supervised employees. Although a minority predicted unsatisfactory work, most inexperienced managers forecast sales success.

One manager predicted unsatisfactory sales work but said that "our Negro radio repairman does excellent work." Another, predicting satisfactory in-store selling, based his forecast on the fact that he already had a Negro successfully selling electrical appliances door-to-door on a commission basis (although apparently only in Negro neighborhoods). Another predicted satisfactory performance on the basis of the successful work of Negro salesgirls in the New York branches of the same chain.

One "very satisfactory" prediction was given by a manager who had successfully employed Negro clerical workers and also recently "had a dark Cuban girl (probably some Negro blood) do well in sales work." Another such prediction came from a chain-store manager who had already used Negro salegirls in the Chicago branch. Most of the regular salegirls in the store were Jewish. When the Jewish New Year arrived, the manager put his Negro stock girls behind the counter in order to keep the store open for business, and they "did real well."[3]

Two avowedly "southern" store managers split over their predictions. The one more recently from the South predicted satisfaction, while the other, the less educated of the two, was sure that unsatisfactory work would be done.

Unsatisfactory work was predicted more often by managers of small stores. For example, of six stores in Minneapolis with less than 50 employees each, four managers predicted unsatisfactory work, one mixed, and only one the modal satisfactoriness. Similarly, the manager of the only small St. Paul store predicted mixed work. Conversely, the managers of the three largest stores without previous Negro employees in each city unanimously predicted satisfactory work. The atypicality of the Southerner who predicted satisfactory work is emphasized by the fact that his store was much the smallest of any of those studied.

The 40 inexperienced managers were asked to comment specifically on their predictions of Negro performance. Nearly all of them (85%) did so, many at length. A content analysis of these comments produced the 14 categories shown in Table 3-2. Although many managers gave more than one reason, almost all multiple responses fell in the same broad category: satisfactory, contingent, or unsatisfactory.

Three respondents commented on probable superior performance of Negro salesgirls, 31 mentioned contingencies, and 20 specified adverse factors. These proportions are roughly equivalent to the two predictions of very satisfactory work, the 25 of satisfactory or mixed performance, and the

[3]This man generalized about Negroes when he said that, "in my experience elsewhere, they're either good or no good, no in-betweens. When they're good, they're damn good." Caplow suggests that this dichotomization is probably "a class phenomenon, equivalent to saying that there are middle-class Negroes and lower-class Negroes." Without realizing the dynamics of class stratification, these managers are enthusiastic about Negroes who exemplify the middle-class virtues of sobriety, courtesy, and industriousness. Conversely, they denounce, with the moral indignation that the term "bad Negroes" implies, the carelessness, occasional dishonesty, and irresponsibility that these managers observe in lower-class Negroes.

12 of unsatisfactory work in Table 3-1. The comments reveal clearly the contingency element in the modal prediction of satisfactory work.

Table 3-2
Inexperienced Managers' Reasons for Their Predictions of Negro Sales Performance

REASON FOR PREDICTION	PERCENTAGE OF TOTAL RESPONDENTS
Satisfactory because	
Negro would make the most of the opportunity	9%
Contingent on	
The individual Negro (general)	24
The individual's middle-classness	18
The individual's ability and experience	18
The individual's personality	15
The individual's intelligence	9
The individual's education	6
The department placement	3
Unsatisfactory because	
Our store lacks Negro customers	9
Negroes generally lack	
training	18
experience	9
customer following	9
aggressiveness in selling	3
ability to take criticism	12
Total*	162%
Number of managers giving reasons	34

*Total comes to more than 100% because some respondents gave more than one reason.

The three comments about performance superior to whites included the two respondents who had predicted very satisfactory work and a third who had predicted satisfaction. All three comments were similar: "Negroes would be grateful for the opportunity to do sales work and would therefore work extra hard"; "They would be anxious to do a good job and would probably perform better than average"; and "Right now the intelligent ones go all out on the job." Recognizing the pressure that the job ceiling places on ambitious Negroes, the last respondent predicted that, "if jobs were wide-open for colored people, they would eventually become as lackadaisical as whites."

Although Negroes generally feel the pressure of the job ceiling, this manager thought that only the "intelligent" ones would respond favorably to an above-ceiling position by making the most of it. An emphasis on differences among Negroes is the most striking characteristic of these managers' comments. All but one of the contingent responses are based on the recognition that Negroes differ from one another and that it is, therefore, unrealistic to treat them as a homogeneous group.

The exception is the manager who listed departmental placement as a condition of success. This 3% response is markedly smaller than the 46% of experienced managers who mentioned department placement, training, and supervision. Although inexperienced managers neglected their own role in determining Negro sales performance, they gave six other contingent characteristics of the individual employee that are consistent with the 39% of the experienced managers who stressed careful selection.

There is considerable overlapping between the modal subcategory of "it depends on the individual" and the contingent factors of personality and middle-classness. Specific elaborations on individuality were the following:

> Our experience with Negro salesgirls would probably be mixed just as it is with whites.
> I know enough psychology to know about individual differences.
> Some Negroes are better than some whites.

Personality factors that one manager deemed especially desirable were "interest, ambition, and eagerness to get ahead." The existence of subcultures within the Negro community is recognized in these statements:

> There are two kinds of Negroes, good ones and bad ones.
> My colored girls described one Negro porter as an "ornery Mississippi nigger" and asked me how I could employ such a person. You see, there are two definite classes of Negroes.

The last manager was impressed that his own Negro elevator operators so vigorously separated themselves from the lower-class porter. Middle-class assets include "refinement" (mentioned by three managers), cleanliness (by two), neatness, good grooming, and coming from "a decent home" (by one each).

The remaining contingencies form a second cluster. The inexperienced managers did not differentiate sharply between ability, intelligence, and education. One manager believed that "many Negroes have had the necessary experience." Several respondents referred simply to the fact that Negroes vary in ability. Good English usage was a requirement for one personnel manager who thought that a Negro college graduate might be sufficiently educated to do "O.K." in his "5 and 10 cent" store.

These contingencies disclose that extent to which inexperienced Twin Cities managers thought of Negroes as individuals rather than as a group. The common assertion that white people think of Negroes in stereotyped terms until those whites have had personal experience with them is contradicted by the managers' comparatively sophisticated approach to "racial" differences.

Managers in the third group felt that the average Negro falls short The common assertion that white people think of Negroes in stereotyped stores frequently listed high training and experience requirements. Four of five Minneapolis stores predicting general inadequacy due to lack of training were specialized—three furniture stores, and one men's clothing store. The latter's personnel manager spent some minutes illustrating how much his salesmen have to know about materials, styles, and names of items. The only St. Paul manager who viewed lack of training as an insuperable handicap made his point twice: "Selling is especially difficult here; this store is a tough one to work in because we're a specialty store" (women's clothing).

Closely related to training is the requirement of previous sales experience, which was stressed by two out of three hardware firms and by a women's clothing store ("our standards of experience are so high that few whites can qualify"). Said one of the hardware men:

> A thorough hardware background is essential. Having a college degree doesn't help a bit. We keep thousands of items in stock, and a salesman has to know them all by name. This is such a technical line that it is difficult to find even whites who are qualified.

The experience requirement is a difficult hurdle for Negroes; unable to get specialty sales jobs because of lack of experience, Negroes cannot gain the qualifying experience. At this point the job ceiling produces a vicious circle.

One specialty store steals customers from its competitors by hiring their best salesmen. No Negroes, the manager added, are likely to acquire enough of a personal following to give them much market value. Two other stores hold their sales employees for such long periods of time (for example, 25 years) that those employees build up customer loyalties, which benefit the store.

Even if given a chance, Negroes were expected to be handicapped in securing a personal following. Three St. Paul managers thought of potential clienteles for Negro sales clerks among only "their own kind." The belief of these managers in segregated clerk-customer relationships is unusually conservative for the Twin Cities.

Predictions of difficulty in disciplining Negro sales personnel were frequently based on experience with Negroes in lower job classifications:

> Our janitors refused to do certain types of work which they considered beneath them.
> Our Negro employees resent the floor lady's and even the assistant manager's suggestions, will take orders only from me.
> Negroes can't take criticism of work, often quit when criticized; are a lot of trouble that way.
> Negroes would be liable to misinterpret ordinary customer rudeness as race discrimination, are apt to be touchy.

There is an element of consistency between the "contingent" and the "unsatisfactory" comments. We have already described the "contingent" comments as individualistic and nonracial. While the "unsatisfactory" comments are generalized rather than individualistic, they are seldom "racial" in the sense of inabilities inherent in the Negro race. The modal deficiencies in training and experience are socially determined, and none of the managers concerned about these factors implied any inherent inability to learn the necessary skills. As one furniture-store personnel manager said,

"If Negroes were given the same opportunities, they would be O.K., but they've been handicapped in training and education." When managerial sophistication about Negro abilities does not express itself individualistically, it does so sociologically.

The Twin Cities Pioneers

We have seen that inexperienced managers are surprisingly unprejudiced in their attitudes toward potential Negro salesgirls. These managers foresee possible difficulties, but they are confident that, with proper managerial handling, difficulties could be resolved (or else they would never hire any Negroes).

How do these attitudes compare with the actual experience of the first Twin Cities managers who ever risked placing Negroes in customer-contact positions? By 1949 seven Minneapolis stores had employed Negro salesgirls. Two stores no longer had any but reported on their experience. In St. Paul four stores had Negro salesgirls.[4] A fifth had recently employed its first Negro waitresses in the hope that they would pave the way for Negro salesgirls.[5]

For the evaluation of the personnel managers' experience with Negro salesgirls, the 13 executives were asked, "What has been the quality of the work done by your Negro sales personnel?" and "Did they do much better, better, the same, worse, or much worse than you expected?"

The response categories, already shown in Table 3-1, are subjective. From additional comments, "very satisfactory" seemed to indicate performance superior to that of the average white salesgirl. There is probably some overlapping between "satisfactory" and "mixed," but the latter usually involves some dissatisfaction and is particularly appropriate when some employeess have succeeded and others have not. For instance, a Minneapolis

[4]For experimental purposes a recheck was run on one of these stores and revealed marked divergence between the two officials interviewed. The recheck demonstrated that this part of the survey deals not so much with objective measures of employee ability as with the respondents' subjective evaluations. The managers' estimates are not the experience of a certain number of stores but the reactions to that experience of a certain number of persons. Hence when two persons in the same store evaluate a given experience differently, it seemed best to include both schedules in the tabulations. Averaging the two would give a false picture of medium performance, and there was no justification for discarding one or the other of the two schedules.

[5]While the previous tables listed these ten waitresses as "other service" personnel (since the management of the store so considers them), their "sales" experience will be reported here to broaden our fund of information. This addition seems justified because (1) waitresses are in contact with customers just as salesgirls are and differ little from the fountain girls whom a Minneapolis executive brackets as sales clerks; and (2) these waitresses represented a break in the ceiling for the particular store, although Negroes traditionally held such positions in local hotels and in some restaurants. Hence the waitresses were a test case for further upward mobility.

manager who checked this category commented that "most of our Negro salesgirls have not been too successful, but at present we have one who looks good." He added that "we have not had a representative sample to date" and hesitated to check any category for fear of judging a whole race on the basis of a handful of employees. Similarly, a St. Paul manager had discharged two sales people as unsatisfactory (one "lacked interest" and the other "had an inferiority complex in spite of being well educated; she hesitated to approach customers and therefore was a poor seller"), but he now had a more successful salesgirl.

The "don't know" response came from a young man who had been promoted to personnel manager only one week before the interview and had no basis for judgment.

One manager with "very unsatisfactory" experience reported that his first Negro salesgirl "decided the work was too hard and quit after one month." Shortly thereafter, a second girl was hired, but she never did any work and was fired. The personnel manager did not feel that this experience was conclusive and was willing to give another girl a try sometime. However, this manager reported that her boss, the general manager of the store, "feels that two failures are enough and doesn't want to try any more." Here is the only case in which unsatisfactory experience led to this conclusion. All the other managers who experienced difficulties blamed the inexperience of the individuals involved and planned to continue hiring Negroes. The generally prejudiced atmosphere of the exceptional store is suggested by the manager's report that "our Jewish salesgirls have failed too; they are always too aggressive, so we just don't hire any more."

Two officials of one St. Paul store disagreed about their experience with Negro salesgirls. A female official described the overall performance of her Negro salesgirl as mixed. "At first her work was very good." That "her work has been falling off recently" was attributed to complacency; "at first she was anxious to succeed, but now she feels soo secure." This official ended optimistically with a comment that the girl "is improving in attitude." Two weeks later, a male official stressed the disadvantages of the same experience for the company. Checking "very unsatisfactory," he described the girl's sales as "getting progressively worse," to the point where she was "the lowest selling person in the department with the company losing money on her." He could not understand her poor performance except that "maybe she just can't sell." Since she was consistently "on time, never absent, and devoted to duty," and "seems to have plenty of personality," none of the more obvious qualifications was missing.

This discrepancy between a "mixed" and a "very unsatisfactory" evaluation of the same job performance is correlated with differences in the general orientation of the two managers. The woman was consistently sympathetic toward Negroes, whereas the man was one of the few Twin Cities managers who displayed stereotyped prejudice against Negroes.

Thus the evaluations by the first 13 managers experimenting with Negro sales clerks were highly diversified, ranging all way from great satisfaction to equally great dissatisfaction.

Unfortunately we have no way of comparing these evaluations of Negro salesgirls with experience with white trainees. Presumably the latter would be rated as mixed over the years. Managers who had tried only one Negro salesgirl might have either a very good or a very bad experience. The larger the number of employees, the less extreme the average evaluation was likely to be. Despite the diversity of initial experiences, the central tendency of the managers was to report that their Negro salesgirls' work was satisfactory.

Predictions versus Experience

I had expected advance predictions about Negro sales performance to be more pessimistic than actual experience. This hypothesis can be tested in two ways: (1) How do inexperienced managers' predictions compare with experienced managers' reports? and (2) How do the latter's experiences compare with their own prior expectations?

Table 3-1 (p. 28) shows that inexperienced managers are not significantly more pessimistic. Seldom extremely optimistic and never extremely pessimistic, their predictions cluster in the middle range of possible opinions. The specific experience of the 13 employers of Negro salesgirls was more often either better or worse than what the nonemployers predicted would happen in their own stores. Nevertheless, the experienced and inexperienced managers had, on the average, substantially the same views of Negro sales ability. This agreement indicates that Twin Cities nonemployers were not generally prejudiced against Negroes on the ground of innate inability. Even the 30% in Table 3-1 who predicted unsatisfactory sales work did so chiefly on the basis of the social handicaps that Negroes face.

The experienced managers reported similarly that most of their pioneers lived up to managerial expectations. For five managers, the girls did the same as expected, for four the experience was better, and for three it was worse (omitting one man who was so new that he could not report prior expectations).

When managers recalled how they had expected their Negro salesgirls to work out, these men kept in mind their planned precautions. As one manager said, "Under those circumstances, failure was practically impossible." Consequently, when his first salesgirl performed satisfactorily, he listed her work as "the same as" he had expected.

For some managers this second evaluation was a way of congratulating themselves for their skill in prognosis and in management of the placement problem. One manager who said that his Negro employees' work was worse than he had expected qualified his remark with the apology that his workers "were inexperienced" and involved so few cases that he hated to check any category. A respondent whose evaluation of his Negro salesgirl's performance matched his prediction added that she "at first did much better than we expected."

The experienced managers' modal evaluations of (1) "satisfactory" performance and (2) the "same as expected" are consistent with experience elsewhere.

In the North many important business corporations employ Negroes side by side with whites, and on their clerical staffs as well as elsewhere. The general verdict is that Negro workers are as good as other workers, that when they have the same training and the same opportunity they do quite as satisfactory a job (MacIver, 1948).

The managers' evaluations of Negro sales performance are reinforced by customer evaluations in New York City in the same postwar years.

The 69 people who reported buying from a Negro clerk were asked: "Did she do as good a job as a white person would have done?" Seventy-nine percent thought the Negro clerk had behaved in the same manner as a white clerk would have, four percent thought she had done a worse job, and 17% thought she had done a better job (Saenger and Gilbert, 1950).

Almost all the New York customers found Negro salesgirls no different from white clerks. My comparison between actual and predicted performance is, of course, different from the one used by Saenger and Gilbert. Nevertheless, the results of the comparisons coincide, since neither group of respondents was surprised by its actual experience.

In general, then, the pioneer Negro salesgirls in the Twin Cities (as in New York) performed as adequately as had been expected by the men who hired them—and as would have been predicted by most of the men who did not.

The Breakthrough Office Workers

Four Minneapolis stores had full-time Negro clerical workers in 1949, and one store assigned a girl to combined typing and stock work. One manager called his experience with Negro clerical workers "very satisfactory," three "satisfactory," and one "mixed." Since these managers tended to hire Negro clerical workers in pairs, nine girls were employed in the five stores. The very satisfied respondent reported that his stenographers "try hard to make the best of the opportunity." A satisfied manager said, "We have had enough experience to *know* that they do a good job," but he added that he was not yet sure about his Negro salesgirls (whom he had given a "mixed" evaluation). The manager who gave a "mixed" evaluation of his clerical workers commented that "it depends on the person —I can't say it has been satisfactory on the whole—the girls we've hired have had handicaps in family background."

There is a close correlation between the managers' experience with office girls and their prior expectations. All four with full-time girls had expected satisfactory work. The two managers whose girls proved satisfactory said it was what they had expected. The very satisfactory experience of another manager was better than he had expected, and the mixed experience of the fourth was "on the whole" worse than he hoped for (with the exception of one newly employed girl, who was doing satisfactory work, "the same as" expected).

Specific comments about prior expectations amplify these responses. The "better" performance was turned in by two "above-average girls, one a high-school honor student," who "grasped the job pretty fast" in spite of the fact that neither had had any clerical experience, though both had just finished high-school commercial courses. One man who had expected satisfactory performance had taken the precaution of hiring the girl first as a maid, then upgrading her to elevator operator, and finally moving her into the office to operate the addressograph and mailing machines. The manager with mixed experience bemoaned the fact that "five of the six Negro stenographers we've employed over the last ten years have used the job as a stepping-stone to marriage and haven't stayed with it long enough to be of much value to the company."

The prior expectation of satisfactory performance of clerical work and the actual fulfillment of that expectation by the majority of Negroes hired resembles the satisfactory experience of the larger number of stores who have employed Negroes as salesgirls.

Table 3-3 indicates how this experience with Negro clerical workers compares with the predictions of the remaining 46 respondents.

Table 3-3
Inexperienced and Experienced Managers' Estimates of Negro Clerical Performance

	TYPE OF ESTIMATE	
CLERICAL PERFORMANCE	PREDICTIONS BY INEXPERIENCED MANAGERS	EVALUATIONS BY EXPERIENCED MANAGERS
Very satisfactory	2%	20%
Satisfactory	63	60
Mixed	24	20
Unsatisfactory	4	0
Very unsatisfactory	0	0
Don't know	7	0
Total	100%	100%
Number of managers	46	5

Critical ratio = .68, probability < .50 for satisfactory categories combined.

Table 3-3 shows that a majority predicted satisfactory achievement for potential Negro clerical workers. These predictions correspond closely with the actual experience of the five pioneering stores. However, the managers of the four stores with full-time clerical employees had expected 100%

satisfaction. The greater optimism of these managers was the result of both the selective nature of the group, who voluntarily took the initiative in hiring Negro clerical workers, and the fact that the managers responded to the expectation question in terms of the particular well-qualified individuals whom they had hired and in whom they had confidence.

In general, the predominant correspondence between prior expectation and actual experience on the one hand, and between the nonemployers' predictions and the employers' experience on the other, echoes the findings about the pioneering Negro salesgirls. These two sets of predictions, though based on above-ceiling work that requires two different kinds of skill, show that nonemployers rarely deprecate the ability of Negroes to perform jobs for which they have not been hired.

So far, I have discussed the close correspondences *within* each job category. If, however, we compare the levels of expectation and experience for the two fields, we find a noticeable discrepancy. Satisfactory performance was predicted or reported for clerical work by 65-80% of managers, but for sales by only 47-54%. In short, clerical breakthroughs seemed more promising than sales breakthroughs.

This finding surprised me, because I had assumed that clerical work requires more skill and carries higher prestige than sales. In specialized stores, the reverse may be true; sales may require years of familiarity with the merchandise and of skill in approaching customers. On the other hand, in answering this question, the managers may have gone beyond evaluating the minimal qualifications necessary for handling a retail counter (as in a variety store) to invoke their own fears of negative customer reactions to Negro salesgirls (see Chapter 5). Because selling is an interpersonal relationship, the managers' pessimism about customers may have acted adversely on their evaluation of Negro sales ability.

The inexperienced managers commented less often about predicted Negro clerical ability than about sales ability. The following comments are typical. One favorable remark was that "they probably would make every effort to do well." Several contingent comments were these: on ability, "There are just as many qualified Negroes as whites"; on education, "After all, they go to the same high schools as the whites"; on personality, "Some Negroes are conscientious and try hard"; and on the individual in general, "There's no difference between white and Negro." The few unfavorable comments included the remark that "clerical jobs require a great deal of skill—more than most Negroes have" and a report that a store's Chicago branch had employed Negro stenographers who had been "very unsatisfactory—they are less exact, make more errors." This report concluded that "the average Negro high-school graduate of a business course is not as well qualified as the average white." This predicted handicap in home background (exhibited especially in poor English usage) was echoed by an employer experienced with Negro stenographers.

One rechecked store had had several Negro applicants for clerical jobs but had hired none. The abilities of the average applicant were evaluated contradictorily by different managers: "Qualified Negro applicants are the exception, but qualified whites are the rule" versus "Only the best qualified Negroes have applied, whereas many unqualified whites apply." Another manager believed "a few" Negroes were "O.K. in typing ability" but pointed out that Negroes were automatically excluded from his office staff because his selections were always made from his all-white sales force.

The experience of Twin Cities store managers in the employment of pioneering Negroes above the job ceiling as both sales clerks and office workers was generally satisfactory. However, contrary to my initial hypothesis, employers who did not hire Negroes in these occupational classifications did not assume that Negroes were incapable of learning or performing the necessary skills. Hence, the failure of the managers to hire Negroes must have been the result of fears about repercussions from their white employees or their white customers.

Chapter 4

Fears and Realities—The Reactions of White Employees to Negro Breakthroughs

I expected employers who hired Negroes to experience few repercussions from their white employees and employers who had not hired Negroes to predict employee resistance.

This hypothesis was based on research elsewhere. According to Stouffer (1949), "perhaps the most illuminating piece of data coming out of the study" of Negro and white World War II soldiers was this finding:

> ... The closer men approached to the mixed-company organization, the less opposition there was to it. That is, men actually in a company containing a Negro platoon were most favorable toward it, men in larger units in which there were no mixed companies were least favorable, while men in all-white companies within a regiment or division containing mixed companies held intermediate opinions. When we note that the proportion of men having no experience with mixed companies who say "they would dislike the arrangement very much" is almost exactly the same (62%) as the 2/3 proportion of white enlisted men in mixed companies who were previously noted as reporting retroactively that they were initially opposed to the idea, we can get some conception of the revolution in attitudes that took place among these men *as a result of enforced contacts* (emphasis added).

White soldiers who fought alongside Negro platoons changed their attitudes markedly.

> Both white officers and fellow enlisted men reported that the white and Negro soldiers got along well together (93% of the officers and 60% of the enlisted men said "very well"; everyone else said "fairly well"), in spite of the fact that two-thirds of each group had begun, according to their own restrospective reports, with relatively unfavorable attitudes toward serving in a mixed company. In a similar fashion, the bulk of both groups (77%) reported that their feeling had become more favorable since serving in the same unit with Negro soldiers (Stouffer, 1949).

This wartime research shows that white soldiers with misgivings about equal-status contacts with Negroes were pleasantly surprised by their actual experience. Other studies show similarly changed attitudes in different settings. For example, among merchant seamen of the National Maritime

Union, ". . . it was discovered that the more often white crews had shipped with Negroes, the less prejudiced they were, regardless of their previous geographical origin" (Brophy, 1946).

A nationwide study of business and industry found that employee repercussions were often feared but seldom materialized.

> The managements indicated they had been greatly concerned about the reaction of present employees to having Negro co-workers in their ranks and thought it only realistic to recognize that . . . longstanding prejudices were involved. The majority of these companies found from experience that the anticipated show of prejudice had been greatly overestimated and that the incidence of friction and other unpleasantness in biracial relationships was not great and was manageable where it occurred . . . (Norgren and others, 1959).

Star, Williams, and Stouffer interpreted the Army combat situation as particularly favorable to success because contact was occupational rather than social in nature and lacked the sensitive issue of Negro men interacting with white women (Norgren and others, 1959). Even though participants in integrated housing projects are subject to both social and heterosexual contact with members of the other races, many of the projects have been similarly successful despite initially hostile attitudes of participants. For example, Merton's study (1949) of a Pittsburgh housing project found that

> there is some interpersonal friction here as elsewhere. But in a community made up of equal numbers of the two races, fewer than a fifth of the whites and less than a third of the Negroes report that this friction occurs between members of *different* races. By their own testimony, it is largely confined to disagreements *within* each racial group. Yet only one in 25 whites initially *expected* relations between the races in this community to run smoothly, whereas five times as many expected serious trouble, the remainder anticipating a tolerable, if not altogether pleasant, situation. Upon reviewing their actual experience, three of every four of the most apprehensive whites subsequently found that the "races got along fairly well," after all.

These studies of military, marine, industrial, and housing situations generally find that inter-racial friction is feared by both rank-and-file whites and their superiors. But under proper conditions this friction fails to materialize, and experience with inter-racial cooperation actually improves white attitudes toward the minority group.

Inexperienced Managers' Predictions of Their White Salesgirls' Reactions

Were the inexperienced store managers in the Twin Cities as skeptical of rank-and-file reactions to integration as Army officers had been in World War II? In order to answer this question, the managers were asked how they thought their other employees would react to the employment of Negro sales personnel.

Table 4-1

Inexperienced and Experienced Managers' Estimates of White Employees' Reactions to Negro Salesgirls

EMPLOYEE REACTION	TYPE OF ESTIMATE	
	PREDICTIONS OF INEXPERIENCED MANAGERS	REPORTS OF EXPERIENCED MANAGERS
Favorable		
Very favorable	0%	23%
Favorable, good	4	38
No reaction	25	31
Skepticism changing to acceptance	10	0
Contingent		
Depends on the Negro	13	—
Depends on the department	2	—
Unpredictable	10	—
Unfavorable		
Unfavorable (general)	9	0
Verbal objections	10	8*
Requests for transfer to another department	2	0
Resignations	15**	0
Total	100%	100%
Number of estimates	48	13

Critical ratio = 3.40, probability < .001 for employee reactions as risky (contingent and unfavorable combined).

*"Employee was not here long enough to get a real reaction."

**One of these predictions was qualified with the comment "a few only, not serious."

Table 4-1 shows that most inexperienced managers predicted negative (36%) or uncertain reactions (25%); for these two groups, employee reaction was at best risky. Hence, the typical manager was afraid of what his white employees might do.

Some managers explained the basis of their predictions. One was confident that his employees would react favorably but wanted the advance approval of the department head in order to be sure of sympathetic leadership. Another manager (the only one in either city considering hiring a Negro salesman) predicted no reaction because

> management would set the pace. They'd have to like him. They would cooperate with him and be courteous and friendly just as toward any other salesman. That's company policy.

Another asserted that, "where the employer takes a strong stand, the employees change their attitudes fast." Four of the five managers clarifying predictions of "no reaction" emphasized managerial leadership in setting the stage for Negro breakthroughs. The exceptional manager felt that employee reactions could be predicted from present acceptance of Negro stock girls: "They get along well now at our store Christmas parties"; this acceptance did not surprise the manager because "in St. Paul they go to school together, swim together, and are used to each other."

Comments about individual characteristics included one on appearance, five on personality, and two on ability. Two managers whose major predictions were unfavorable said they would want to place Negroes in isolated departments to avoid employee trouble. Since there were no isolated departments in those two stores, the managers could not employ any Negroes.

Managers who exhibited "skepticism changing to acceptance" commented that white salesgirls "would be skeptical until the Negro had proven her ability to do the job." Another said,

> I've seen bigots on our staff get to know and be buddies with our present Negro employees. The problem is not insoluble.

One "unpredictable" respondent revealed:

> Employee attitudes don't make any difference to us. We don't ask them before we do things. We just go ahead if we think it's a good thing to do.

To him, possible negative reactions were not a proper basis for deciding policy. Another employer had had previous favorable experience but hesitated to generalize from it:

> I told [my white employees] to accept the Negro stock girls, so they did, of course. But salesgirls are a different, higher type of people—I might say one thing and they might do differently.

Unfavorable predictions included "a lot of ill feeling" and a "social boycott" of the Negro sales person. Two inexperienced employers expected their employees to object to integration if they were asked in advance:

> I asked them last fall and got some feeling against it, especially from the girls.
> I wouldn't hire any Negroes unless our salesgirls agreed to it in advance. They would probably refuse to work with Negroes, so we wouldn't hire any.

Another manager predicted that his employees would complain "to the union, which would present the grievance to the company," if he hired a Negro salesgirl and added that "we have enough friction as it is with the union." To check on this prediction of trouble from the union, Local No. 2, Retail Clerks Union, A.F.L., was asked whether this store manager had stated accurately the procedure they would follow if members objected to a Negro salesgirl. The official reply from international organizer William Gydesen on behalf of the Twin Cities locals was the following:

> The Retail Clerks Union has never and will not deny membership to Negro sales people. As a matter of fact, we have encouraged it, and in St. Paul in two department stores where Negro sales people are employed, they are members of our Union and are doing a commendable job and are entitled to all the rights and privileges of other sales people.[1]

Thus one store manager foresaw trouble that was unlikely to materialize.

[1] Quoted with permission.

As might be expected, our two southern managers predicted sharp repercussions from their white employees; one estimated that "50% would quit," and the other foresaw "calamity." One pessimistic Northerner reported, "Previously our white maids threatened to quit when we wanted to hire a Negro maid. We couldn't convince them to accept the Negro, so we backed down." This instance was the only one in which white employees interpreted the hiring of a Negro as a threat. to their jobs (as maids might well do in view of the managerial predilection for all-Negro cleaning staffs). The rest of this respondent's comments suggest a general uncertainty about the employment of Negroes that he may have conveyed to the white maids.

One personnel manager, who expected a few white employees to quit, remarked philosophically, "I'm not much worried about that. Some people never change. There are prima donnas who quit due to the whites we hire, too!"

Most inexperienced managers, then, felt queasy about their white employees. Some were sure that trouble would result, and others were uncertain. Only a minority were confident that the sales staffs could be maintained intact in the face of a drastic change in age-old custom.

How White Salesgirls Actually Reacted to Negro Breakthroughs

We have discovered widespread fear and uncertainty among inexperienced managers about employee reactions. In order to find out whether those negative predictions were fulfilled in actual experience, the 13 Twin Cities managers who employed the first Negro salesgirls (including the marginal fountain girls and waitresses) were asked how their white employees reacted. Table 4-1 shows that only one manager's employees reacted unfavorably. Even this reaction was an initial one that might have changed for the better if the employee had not quit a few days later. In another store an initially favorable response changed to resentment when management failed to impose the usual discipline on the new employee. Since this hostility was directed more toward management than the employee, it seems justifiable to describe the initial reaction as favorable. Another qualified report stated that the reaction "was good in the particular departments where we placed them but wouldn't have been in some others." One manager was optimistic about white reactions throughout his store; he stated that "people in the store seem generally receptive" to the idea of Negro salesgirls and that employee attitudes in this respect "are 100% better than they were ten years ago."

Whereas more than one-third of the inexperienced managers predicted distinctly unfavorable employee reactions, only one actual experience out of 13 was unfavorable. And this one was unfavorable not because of the girl's race but because of her personal characteristics. Few employers like to embark on unpredictable ventures, and the addition of the "contingent" category to the "unfavorable" means that three-fifths of the inexperienced managers foresaw enough trouble with their white employees to discourage those managers from hiring Negro sales persons. This obervation confirms our original hypothesis that employers who have not hired Negroes fear there might be employee resistance.

The contrast between fears and realities is reinforced by the before-and-after views of the breakthrough managers. Eight of the 13 found that their white employees reacted better than expected. Most managers had expected the worst and were much relieved when their employers gave no observable negative reaction.

Only one manager found that his white employees' reactions were worse than he had anticipated. The reactions found by the remaining four managers were just as favorable as they had predicted. Predictions of favorable reactions were based on careful exploration or manipulation of employee attitudes. These precautions ranged from one personnel man who "talked to the people in the department ahead of time and found that they had no objections" to another who "made it clear ahead of time that if the employees didn't want to work with Negroes they could voluntarily resign." More common was the moderate approach of explaining why the company had decided to employ a Negro sales person and announcing that the company expected the new girl to be given a friendly reception. One personnel manager reported that her employees "followed instructions nicely."

The managers of two Minneapolis stores combined inquiry and instruction. These men discovered department heads who were receptive to having Negro employees and had them "pass the word around to make sure there would be no negative responses." Subsequent precautions were usually skipped. For example, the store that hired the largest number of Negro salesgirls "paved the way only in the case of the first such employee—since then, we have placed Negroes just like any white."

All but one of the Minneapolis employers took such precautions and hence were confident of success. Significantly, the manager who made no special preparation was one of the two whose employees reacted better than he had expected: "We thought there might be a little resentment, but the Negroes stick to their jobs, so there has been no animosity." The other pleasantly suprised respondent was "pretty sure it would be O.K." in view of the preparations he had made, but he added that "you never can tell how human beings are going to react." Similarly, two St. Paul stores who made no preparatory efforts "expected slight resistance," and a third "had no idea what would happen, although generally Negroes seem to be taken at face value in St. Paul."

On the whole, there were hardly any employee repercussions to the integration of Negroes.[2] A few negative reactions were directed not against race as such but against personal characteristics or managerial favoritism. Employees accepted changes regardless of whether advance preparations were made. However, many managers felt that special precautions insured against trouble. Selecting sympathetic department heads and announcing firm company policy were subjectively useful to the managers. Taking such steps provided them with peace of mind, which is an important consideration since many employers fail to hire Negroes because those employers fear employee reactions.

Some experts recommend that management provide firm leadership in new situations. For example, Haas and Fleming (1946) list the following as essential ingredients of an integration program:

1. *Self-education and self-conviction on the part of management and policy-making and policy-enforcing officials.*
2. *The taking of a firm position by management once it has been decided to adopt the new policy.* Experience has shown . . . that nearly every strike by white workers against the introduction of Negroes may be traced to the lack of a firm stand by the employer or, even worse, hints by responsible management representatives that management itself was not "solid" behind the new program.

Similarly, Dean and Rosen (1955) emphasize the power of institutional leaders to initiate change.

Leaders who control the operating practices of an institution or social environment can establish intergroup policies and practices for that environment within a wide range of community customs. These new practices, even if they differ from the generally accepted prior practices, then become the established and accepted customs to which participants conform.

This power to establish new policies is especially influential over the subordinate personnel of an institution.

Where there are clear lines of authority or administrative control, people tend to go along with the rules and regulations that are passed down from the top, even when their initial feelings about these regulations may not be favorable (Dean and Rosen, 1955).

One institution with clear lines of authority is the Army. During initial experiments with integration,

[2]The reaction of white employees depends on the extent to which the introduction of Negroes threatens the jobs of the existing labor force. If, for example, Negroes are brought in as strikebreakers to replace white employees or are hired in traditionally "white" jobs during a period of general unemployment and thereby impair the right of existing employees to nominate relatives and friends for scarce job openings, the reaction can be expected to be negative. The Twin Cities breakthroughs occurred under relatively unthreatening circumstances.

. . . in at least some . . . cases there was careful selection of officers and orientation of the white troops. . . . A platoon commander from Texas said: "We all expected trouble. Haven't had any. One reason may be that we briefed the white boys in advance—told them these men were volunteers coming up here to fight, and that we wouldn't stand for any foolishness" (Stouffer, 1949).

These sources credit management leadership with a major role in preventing inter-racial friction. They recommend the establishment of an authoritative relationship between management and white employees in order to insure the successful integration of Negroes.

Some Twin Cities employers abandoned this leadership by asking white employees whether Negroes should be hired. This procedure often evokes resistance. Goodwin Watson (1946) reports that "one department store, for example, polled its employees to find out whether they would be willing to have Negro girls as clerks. A large majority of the white girls objected and management found its hands. tied."

Robin Williams (1947) calls polling the worst possible way of introducing minority-group members into new activities. Three possible methods are the following:

(a) gradual introduction of selected individuals, with a minimum prior discussion or announcement;
(b) statement that the minority will be introduced, accompanied by a considerable volume of information, exhortation, and discussion prior to the change itself;
(c) polling, or otherwise determining wishes of the majority group in advance of the change—the results being understood to constitute a binding decision.

Procedure (a) will be most effective in securing acceptance with a minimum of conflict, in cases in which there are relatively tolerant initial attitudes in the majority population.

Procedure (b) will be the more effective method in the case of populations having relatively strong initial prejudice.

Procedure (c) will almost always be the least effective of the three methods named.

Opinion polls usually uncover widespread opposition to integration. Williams blames this occurrence on the abandonment of definite leadership:

Conflict between persons of different identifiable groups is the more likely when there is *no clear definition of the situation*, especially with regard to detailed patterns of "appropriate" personal behavior (emphasis mine).

Merton (1949) cites, under the title of "The Self-fulfilling Prophecy," the importance of situational definitions, first proposed by W. I. Thomas (in Merton, 1949) in the theorem "If men define situations as real, they are real in their consequences." The disadvantage of polling white employees lies in the fact that management thereby asks employees to define the situation for themselves. In the absence of preconceived opinions, employees fall back on latent prejudices that our culture implants in the subconscious mind of the average citizen. By calling these latent prejudices into play, the poll precipitates a psychological "set" opposed to the introduction of Negroes. For such reasons, Dean and Rosen (1955) flatly oppose polling employees about desegregation:

> Polling those involved in advance of an intergroup change calls forth many more negative reactions than will actually occur if the change is undertaken as matter-of-factly as any other change that might be instituted.

But submerged prejudice is not the only ingredient of the American mind. Our national tradition boasts about equal opportunity and fair play. This American Creed creates widespread ambivalence in white Northerners.

In the Twin Cities, initial attitudes were largely vague and unformed— neither openly prejudiced nor openly tolerant. "In all situations where there is ambivalence and uncertainty of direction the resolution displayed by the leader is of crucial importance" (MacIver, 1948). White retail employees were so ambivalent that they could easily be swayed by leadership from any quarter. The question was whether leadership would be exerted by management itself, or whether management would leave a vacuum in which an overtly prejudiced individual could crystallize opposition to Negroes.

Management leadership appropriate to situations of indifferent equilibrium" (MacIver) may be exerted by what Watson (1947) calls the "*fait accompli* method." Saenger and Gilbert point out that, "while many people are opposed to social innovations, few will actively fight them." Ambivalent or even prejudiced persons will usually accept a Negro once he is installed by management.

The definitiveness of a change in company policy can be symbolized to white employees by the sharpness of the break with the past. For example, Norgren (1959) found that some companies "deliberately hired dark-skinned Negroes initially to demonstrate that they were not equivocating about their policy of Negro employment." Similarly, the first few Negroes employed above the old job ceiling were assigned to jobs "completely disassociated with traditional Negro work." The very conspicuousness of those breakthroughs dramatized the managerial policy change better than a flurry of directives could have done.

World War II noncommissioned officers who had served with Negroes in adjacent platoons voted overwhelmingly in favor of the degree of interracial relationship that they had actually experienced: 89% favored the *fait accompli* (Negro platoons in the same company), only 1% voted for greater integration (mixed platoons), while the remaining 14% favored greater segregation (Stouffer, 1949). Opposition to a *fait accompli* was even less likely in the Twin Cities of the far North than in an army containing many Southerners.

A clear statement of management policy sharpens the *accompli* aspect of subsequent or associated action and aids in securing favorable definition of the situation. If an employer notifies his employees that he expects a Negro worker to be accepted, that acceptance is almost certain to ensue. The crisis point of indeterminateness may be successfully passed by means of a statement that hiring Negroes is not just an experiment to see how employees will react but a fixed new policy.

Once the initial crisis point is passed, the Negro's status is usually safe. "Even Southern-born workers, although they usually tend to display much more race prejudice than others, have had to become accustomed to working with Negroes" (Myrdal, 1944). MacIver points out that "the experience of working side by side with Negroes leads to habituation on the part of the white workers that weakens the initial opposition." This process was reported by a Minneapolis employer of a Negro office clerk. "When I first hired this girl as an elevator operator, I got some objections because she was very black, but it took only two or three weeks to get accepted, and she's 'one of the girls' now." The same process occurred on a broader scale at the Winchester Arms plant in New Haven:

> . . . Once the decision was carried into effect to employ Negroes in all capacities for which they showed fitness, the policy proved workable, so much so that some of the chief opponents became its stoutest defenders. . . . All persons who dealt with this problem, including the personnel managers and government officials interviewed, agreed that nothing is so important as a firm position on the part of management (MacIver, 1948).

The findings of the Pittsburgh housing project provide a summary of the role of leadership in the integration process: "Under *appropriate institutional and administrative conditions*, the experience of interracial amity can supplant the fear of interracial conflict" (Merton, 1949). In other words, if managers manage, success can be practically guaranteed.

Inexperienced Managers' Predictions about White Office Workers' Reactions

I assumed that office workers were much like salesgirls and that managers would report the same fears and realities for both types of employees. Table 4-2 confirms this assumption. The two sets of inexperienced managers are not identical, since those with sales breakthroughs had yet to hire Negro office workers. Nevertheless, the general pattern for employees' reactions in the office is almost identical with the salesgirl reactions.

Most inexperienced managers predicted unfavorable or contingent responses. Only a minority were confident of favorable reactions (most often in the form of no reaction at all). On the whole, therefore, managers feared possible negative reactions in both types of white-collar jobs.

Table 4-2
Inexperienced and Experienced Managers' Estimates of White Employees' Reactions to Negro Office Workers

	TYPE OF ESTIMATE	
EMPLOYEE REACTION	PREDICTIONS OF INEXPERIENCED MANAGERS	REPORTS OF EXPERIENCED MANAGERS
Favorable		
Very favorable	2%	0%
Favorable, good	2	0
No reaction	28	100
Skepticism changing to acceptance	8	0
Contingent		
Depends on the Negro	14	0
Depends on the department	2	0
Unpredictable	11	0
Unfavorable		
Unfavorable (general)	23	0
Verbal objections	4	0
Change departments	0	0
Resignations	8	0
Total	102%	100%
Number of estimates	53	4

Critical ratio = 2.33, probability = < .05 for employee reactions as not risky (favorable).

The comments of the inexperienced employers varied greatly. Three managers asserted that office people are "more tolerant than sales persons" or are "pretty open-minded." Two believed that placement would be particulary easy if the Negro were light-complexioned. One manager thought it would be "O.K. only in a large office with 40 or 50 girls (we have only one that big)" and remarked that "girls are funnier than men that way." One of the few vehement managers said, "I just wouldn't have any Negroes in the office; I want them out on the floor of the store where they can be watched all the time." Another manager reluctantly predicted "coldness, lack of understanding, and fear of the strangeness at first" and apologized with the explanation that "it's something we're not used to."

How White Office Workers Reacted to Negro Breakthroughs

The first Negro clerical breakthroughs occurred in three stores with full-time workers and one with a part-time worker. Three managers reported no reaction from white employees, and one reported an initial skepticism that changed to acceptance. The skepticism occurred when the office girl was originally hired as an elevator operator. When she was promoted, no negative reaction took place "because the office employees had already accepted her as an individual." Because we are concerned with employee reaction to the integration of Negroes above the ceiling, this case must also be classified as "no reaction," and thus the experience of the four stores is the same.

The three managers with full-time office workers were generally unanimous in having expected no reaction. Indeed, one manager said that "we would have been disappointed to get any. Most of those things are mental anyway." This expectation of successful employee relations reflects the fact that all three had taken the initiative in hiring Negro office workers because those managers were convinced that it was feasible. Since little outside pressure to get Twin Cities stores to employ Negro clerical workers had occurred, these employers would not have pioneered if they had not been confident of favorable office reactions.

These three men were an exception to the general rule that managers fear negative employee reactions. Most managers who hired Negro sales-girls under pressure had been fearful of the results. Curiously, even managers experienced with Negroes in one job category were fearful when they made predictions for another.

Table 4-3

Managers' Predictions of White Employees' Reactions to a New Breakthrough from Previous Experience with a Different White-collar Breakthrough

PREDICTED REACTION OF WHITE EMPLOYEES TO NEW BREAKTHROUGH	BASIS OF PREDICTION	
	PREVIOUS BREAKTHROUGH REACTION OF WHITE SALES EMPLOYEES	PREVIOUS BREAKTHROUGH REACTION OF WHITE CLERICAL EMPLOYEES
Better than before	1	—
The same as before	3½*	1
Risky	1½*	1
Worse than before	7	0
Total	13	2

*One dual prediction divided between these categories.

Table 4-3 shows that over half of the employers who had experienced sales breakthroughs that were without incident predicted negative reactions from the office staffs. Other respondents were not sure what would happen. Only three were confident that their success in introducing Negro workers into sales departments could be duplicated in the office. The only manager with "unfavorable" sales experience had not been deterred by it but predicted future success in the office, just as he indicated his intention to try again in sales. One of the two respondents who had had "no reaction" in the office thought that his sales force was unpredictable. Thus, of 15 respondents with experience in one category, only four predicted that other skilled employees would react the same way the first group had when confronted with a Negro colleague.

Managers who had employed Negro salesgirls made these comments:

Office girls have more status, and hence would be offended more by a Negro. Upgrading would be more of a breaking down of barriers. Office work involves closer contact, is more confining.

Office people are more skilled and harder to replace than sales clerks. We'd be taking too great a risk to hire a Negro, because the store couldn't get along if the white office girls quit.

There is closer contact among office workers; they go out to lunch together, etc. It might cause trouble.

I wouldn't want to take the chance of upsetting the office force.

On the other hand, one optimistic manager reported that the office force reacted satisfactorily when Mexican stenographers were introduced. And another manager reasserted that "the reaction of the employees reflects the management's attitude. If management makes its own stand clear, the employee will go along."

The findings for both sales and clerical work indicate widespread managerial uncertainty about the reactions of white employees if Negroes are to be either hired above the job ceiling or upgraded above it. There was almost no evidence in the experience of actual Twin Cities employers to justify this apprehensiveness. Nevertheless, even employers who had successfully employed Negro sales or clerical help feared what had not been tried. Even satisfied employers hesitated to hire Negroes in the alternate classification lest some new factor disturb their employees. Despite such provocative employer uncertainty, white employees seldom reacted negatively. Despite the danger that such fears might have constituted "self-fulfilling prophecies," those fears proved substantially groundless. The "real consequence" (Thomas) of these prophecies was that managers considered them sufficient reason to refuse skilled employment to Negroes until outside pressure became too strong to resist any longer.

Chapter 5

Fears and Realities—Customer Reactions to Pioneering Negro Salesgirls

In deciding whether to hire Negro applicants for clerical jobs, the only fear involving race is how the existing office staff will react. But when Negro sales clerks are considered, the customers must also be considered.

Inexperienced Managers' Predictions of Customer Reactions

If managers are afraid they may not be able to control their own employees, how much more must they fear customers, who are free to take their trade elsewhere. Where success is measured in rising or falling sales, the customer is necessarily king. The whole purpose of the retail advertising that fattens metropolitan newspapers at the middle of every week is to lure the customer in the front door. If he is then lost because of a dark-skinned salesgirl, the store loses its function as a provider of merchandise and services to customers. Better not to risk the loyalty of the customers that the store already has. Better not to alter the image that makes the important first impression on new customers. Especially when there are so few potential Negro customers who might take the place of offended white ones. Customers, then, are the key to the success or failure of competitive free enterprise. Hence, we should expect managerial anxieties to center around customer reactions.

Table 5-1 shows that inexperienced managers are indeed less confident of favorable customer response (only 28%) than they were of favorable employee response (39% and 40% for sales and office reactions). More-over, loss of customers, the most frequent prediction, is the most damaging threat that could be imagined. Customer loss is predicted more often (23%) than loss of sales employees or office workers (15% and 8%).

Comments on these predictions were numerous. One optimistic respondent spoke appreciatively of the Joint Committee on Employment Opportunity's "lists of customers who favor Negro employees" (see Chapter 8). Another recalled experience in the remote past with a Negro stock man who had occasionally helped sell sporting goods and whom a number of customers had preferred to other salesmen. And a mobile chain-store manager said:

I've been in 11 cities for this firm, and St. Paul is less prejudiced than most of them. This is a multiple-nationality town, a factory town where different groups are used to working side by side, a friendly town.

Table 5-1

Inexperienced and Experienced Managers' Estimates of White Customers' Reactions to Negro Salesgirls

CUSTOMER REACTION	PREDICTIONS OF INEXPERIENCED MANAGERS	REPORTS OF EXPERIENCED MANAGERS
Favorable		
Gain of Negro customers	5%	6%
Expression of approval	3	38
No reaction	12	38
Surprise changing to acceptance	8	0
Contingent		
Depends on the Negro	12	0
Depends on the department	2	0
Depends on the customer	2	0
Depends on competitors' employment practices	3	0
Unpredictable	11	0
Unfavorable		
Expressions of disapproval	9	19
Choice of a white salesgirl	11	0
Loss of customers to competing stores	23	0
Total	**101%**	**101%**
Number of estimates*	**65**	**16**

Critical ratio 3.98, probability < .001 for customer reactions as at least risky (contingent and unfavorable combined).

*Estimates total more than the number of respondents because several managers gave complex responses. For example, all three experienced managers who received expressions of disapproval also received expressions of approval.

A long-time resident of Minneapolis observed that "there seems to be a general trend toward the acceptance of Negroes on the basis of individual ability." An employer of Negro clerical workers agreed that "opposition is diminishing year by year. A lot of it is in the store owners' minds, not really there in the customers!" Despite a southern-born manager's estimate that "at present" 50% of his Minneapolis customers would subjectively disapprove of Negro clerks, he admitted that the trend "seems to be toward greater customer acceptance, and in five or ten years they will probably be more used to it." Two other managers recognized that, "if it was general practice throughout the city, the customers would get used to the idea."

One hardware store's customers were so attached to the store that they were not expected to leave even if they did object to Negro clerks. Moreover, being "good quality clientele, not narrow, they are not apt to object." Another manager emphasized by the twinkle in his eye how convenient it sometimes is to believe that customers are prejudiced: "The reaction would not be as bad as we sometimes like to think."

Some managers thought customer losses might occur but discounted their significance:

One percent of our customers would be unpredictable, but you can't satisfy everyone all the time. After all, we have trouble with *some* of our customers about many aspects of the store.

If any of my customers objected, I'd say, "To hell with them!"

We temporarily lost some customers due to a recent change in company management with the feeling that they (the carriage trade) wouldn't be pampered in the future. But they are coming back now—they always do.

But only stores with a comfortable competitive margin (the first and third) or with a manager who had strong personal convictions about human relations (the second) viewed the possibility of customer loss with anything short of fear and trembling.

Other contingent responses included the report that a southern customer "saw a Negro woman trying on a hat and told me she would never let her husband come in here." But this respondent contended that, "since people accept Negro waiters, Negro sales clerks should be O.K. with most, too" (a psychological nonsequitur, since, in certain circles, waiting on tables is a traditional "Negro job"). One manager thought customer reaction would be "O.K." in hosiery, lingerie, or housewares, but not in the dress department, where the sales woman must fit the dress to the customer.

Six of the ten comments that hinged on the particular Negro specified sales ability as a condition of customer satisfaction, three mentioned personality (for example, "refinement and culture" and "not sticking her neck out"), and the last observed that some Minneapolis colored girls are beautiful enough to increase a store's business from men customers, white as well as Negro.

On the "unfavorable" side were two managers who assumed that Negro clerks would be able to sell only to Negro customers:

Negroes would be at a disadvantage in selling because most of our selling is to other groups.

Negro clerks would be O.K. with our Negro accounts.

A third respondent assumed that the interviewer would agree with him. You would have an aversion to going to a Negro doctor or lawyer even though his ability were equal. It's the same with customers. It's a matter of precedent.

Contrasting attitudes are expressed in the following two quotations:

Probably our Negro customers would be pleased, but maybe even they would prefer being waited on by whites.

Our company gets a lot of business from Negroes. We're careful to treat them especially graciously because they've been mistreated elsewhere. But if we took on a Negro salesman, we'd want him to sell to everyone, not just to Negroes.

Saving Negroes from embarrassment was the protective mood of two employers:

We would be putting the Negro in an embarrassing position to hire one as salesgirl.

I've seen intelligent white women walk into our elevator and say, "Isn't she a black nigger?" intentionally in the hearing of the operator. The 10% of customers who are bigots can make it very uncomfortable for a Negro—shout it out right on the floor of the store. This could lead to tense situations, which would keep me worried about the possibility of razor fights between the salesgirl and the customers.

In the same vein were opinions that "people in this part of the country flare up at the sheer word 'Negro'" and that "you can't force people to like people." Four managers emphasized that the customer aspect "is *the* problem" or that "this might be a *serious* problem," while two remarked that "the customers aren't ready for it" and "we're more apt to have trouble from the customers than from our employees."

Finally, four respondents rejected the relevance of other stores' experience on the ground that "our store is different." One respondent from a furniture store contended that "our class of trade is different here—many of them object to buying from Jewish salesmen," while a recheck respondent from the same store stressed that "this is a small store, more a family store with a personal relationship between customers and salesmen. Hence we would be more apt to lose some sales than would a big department store." Another furniture store's personnel manager ruled out customer acceptance of Negroes because "our salesmen must spend a lot of time with each customer, sometimes as much as four or five hours." And a clothier generalized that, since "Negroes dress too flashily and have a difference in taste from white persons, our customers wouldn't have confidence in a Negro salesman—they would assume he doesn't know much."

The following statement is self-contradictory:

> It depends on the individual employee. If she is refined and cultured, customer reaction would be O.K. It depends entirely on her personality. It's a question here of the character of applicants. Refinement, culture, and education are all they need to qualify. But we wouldn't hire Negroes anyway since most of the customers aren't ready for it.

The modal prediction was pessimistic (loss of customers). Also implying loss of money were predictions that at least some customers would shy away from a Negro salesgirl. And the tone of the "unpredictable" responses indicated that the managers were not eager to experiment on their customers.

How White Customers Reacted to Negro Breakthroughs

Table 5-1 shows that managerial fears of customer repercussions were just as groundless as fears about employees. Only three managers had any unfavorable customer reactions, and each of them received expressions of approval to balance the occasional verbal objections. Not a single manager suffered any financially damaging reactions; no Negro salesgirls were known to have been bypassed for white alternatives, much less any customers actually lost to other stores.

Five managers were applauded directly by customers, and four others were praised in customer letters. One manager noticed that his customers reacted on the basis of their regional background. "The Northerners thought we were being broadminded. The few Southerners among our customers objected." Another manager reported that some customers "were delighted, and others were exceptionally mad and couldn't understand what we were doing." Two employers attributed favorable public reaction to their use of light-skinned Negroes. One of the managers felt that "customers are being educated gradually and later will be ready to accept darker-skinned sales people."

In view of the qualifications made by two managers who reported expressions of approval, the modal reaction must be interpreted as acceptance without comment. Most managers discounted the few objections that they received. None indicated that customer complaints caused any regret that Negro salesgirls had been employed. One who actually got no reaction said that a negative response "wouldn't have influenced him." Characteristically, two personnel officials of a rechecked store split over their report of what happened; the more tolerant one mentioned only expressions of approval, whereas the more prejudiced cited both approval and disapproval. Though expressions of approval and disapproval are weighted the same in Table 5-1, the objections experienced by these managers were far fewer than the plaudits.

A small majority of the experienced managers (eight out of 14) reported that customer reaction was the same as had been expected. A few of them had derived confidence from the breakthrough experience of others:

> We expected (and got) no reaction because the fair-employment idea has been written up so much in the papers.
> Enough other companies were doing it simultaneously so we weren't too worried.
> We didn't expect objections because it's a pretty common thing now in the North.

The other six managers had shared the fears of the inexperienced managers and were pleasantly surprised by the uneventfulness of the outcome. Thus almost half the group (43%) held fears which were disproved by actual experience. The practical importance of fearing the worst can be seen in the comment of one manager, who said that, "if we hadn't thought we could get away with it, we wouldn't have tried."[1]

---

[1]Three Minneapolis respondents without Negro sales clerks had had experience in related categories. Two of these had radio repairmen who belonged to minority groups

Studies of Customer Reactions

Complementing my interviews are two studies in which customers were directly observed and interviewed. A major study was carried out by Saenger and Gilbert in New York City, which is, of course, another northern city, but which has a larger Negro population than the Twin Cities. Sales breakthroughs occurred in New York a year or two earlier than in Minnesota.

For the Saenger and Gilbert study, white customers were interviewed shortly after they had shopped in newly integrated stores. Asked their opinions about Negroes as salesgirls,

> . . . two-fifths . . . failed to express any prejudice. Another fifth approved of Negro sales personnel but showed stereotyped notions concerning Negro inferiority. Two-fifths of the sample were more or less prejudiced. Half of these people—21% of the total group—approved of Negro sales clerks except for certain more "intimate" departments such as clothing, lingerie, food. The remaining 19% were opposed to the hiring of Negro sales personnel generally (Saenger and Gilbert, 1950).

These percentages represent attitudes verbalized as a result of direct questioning. But in actual practice,

> in the department store setting, at least, *prejudicial attitudes* are *not* significantly *correlated with discriminatory behavior.*
>
> Among those who were strongly prejudiced, many said that they would continue to frequent the store and simply turn to the next white clerk if confronted with a Negro. Of the nine people in our sample who said that they would never buy from a Negro, three had actually been observed buying from a Negro less than an hour before they were interviewed. And we cannot be sure even of the remaining six because we do not know how they would have behaved if they had encountered a Negro clerk.
>
> Our study leaves no doubt that prejudiced people, *when asked, will express their prejudices.* It therefore seems wise to introduce Negro sales personnel without prior announcement or questioning of the public. Prior discussion only serves to crystallize opposition. In the event of prior discussion the prejudiced person believes that the choice is left to him, and hence will object. . . .
>
> The presentation of a *"fait accompli,"* however, leads to acquiescence

and were working successfully in the homes of customers:

> We were reluctant to put our Nisei radio repairman on outside, but now the customers prefer him to our others.
>
> People generally accept our Negro radio and television repairman in their homes on the basis of the work done; some even request his services. Just to be sure, the store always asks all customers requesting repair service if they would be willing to take a Negro; the usual answer is "yes."

However, the third respondent found that two crippled and paralyzed white salesgirls whom he had hired met with some customer resistance and generalized that differences of any sort (including skin color) are liable to damage public acceptance.

[2]Prior announcement to employees differs in that management is in a position to influence and control their attitudes. However, management cannot do so in the case of the customer.

by even the most prejudiced. They feel that public opinion is against them and they reconcile themselves in one way or another to the presence of a new group of employees (Saenger and Gilbert, 1950).[2]

In New York City, favorable public opinion was reinforced by public law.

As it happens, social pressure in New York City operates in the direction of less discrimination, of gradual acceptance of Negro white-collar workers in such jobs as sales clerks. This pressure has been powerfully reinforced by the New York State law against discrimination in employment (Saenger and Gilbert, 1950).

Once customers encounter Negro sales clerks, the latent prejudice of the customer tends to evaporate:

> There is . . . some evidence that the hiring of selected Negro clerks actually tends to reduce prejudice. . . . One group of customers did not object to their employment in general. They only wanted them excluded from departments handling "intimate" merchandise. But . . . those who saw Negroes in the food department never objected to their handling food. They only objected to their presence in the clothing departments. Those seeing Negroes in lingerie and clothing departments, on the other hand, objected only to Negroes handling food. Thus the mere presence of Negroes in a specific department appeared to counteract prejudicial expectations, and lead to their acceptance (Saenger and Gilbert, 1950).

The feasibility of Negroes working in departments that sell "intimate" merchandise was rejected by one inexperienced Twin Cities manager, who predicted that "lingerie and corset-fitting departments would be the only two departments in the whole store in which Negroes would be under any serious handicap." However, one Negro saleswoman operated successfully in an infants' wear department of another store.

Conformity to custom is also apparent in the location of the only man among the 17 Twin Cities Negroes classified by managers as doing sales work. This man was in charge of a shoe-repair department (questionably classifiable as a sales position) and was viewed by the store manager as working in "a logical position because the public is used to seeing Negroes working around shoes" (that is, as bootblacks).

In Minneapolis, Augsburg College students interviewed customers during the 1948 Christmas shopping rush. Of 96 customers interviewed, 52 approved of the employment of Negro salesgirls, 22 disapproved, and 23 were indifferent. Indifferent customers argued that "the girls were merely giving them what they asked for." Those opposed to Negro salesgirls gave "startling reasons, such as fear that the Negroes would take over, race riots . . ." (Torstenson, 1948). As in New York, negative correlations were found between education and opposition to Negro salesgirls. In both cities Negro salesgirls were rejected less by women (who do most of the purchasing in American society) than by men, less by high-income people, and less by Jews than by adherents to other religions (see Table 5-2).

In both Minneapolis and New York, therefore, direct study of customers shows that they are mostly favorable or indifferent to Negro salesgirls (as the experienced Twin Cities managers suggested). Only in the minds of inexperienced managers are customer reactions to be feared. Customers are actually more interested in being waited on than in the color of the salesgirl's skin.

Table 5-2

White Customers' Attitudes toward Negro Salesgirls, by Religious Affiliation*

ATTITUDE TOWARD NEGRO SALESGIRLS	RELIGIOUS AFFILIATION		
	PROTESTANT	CATHOLIC	JEWISH
Favorable	56.5%	57.6%	45.5%
Indifferent	15.2	18.2	45.5
Opposed	28.3	24.2	9.1
Total	100.0%	100.0%	100.1%
Number of customers	46	33	11

*Torstenson (1948), Minneapolis only. Cited with the author's permission.

To summarize, almost all inexperienced managers thought customer reaction was risky, whereas almost all the actual experience was favorable. Even the experienced group often expected customer reaction to be worse than it was, whereas none found it worse than expected. Moreover, customer opinions and managerial opinions about customer opinions differ sharply. For instance, only 22% of our Minneapolis managers predicted favorable customer reaction, whereas 77% of the customers interviewed in the same city either favored using Negro sales people or were indifferent. The discrepancy between fears and actualities widens in practice because prejudiced attitudes are liable to be suppressed or even revised when confronted with a Negro salesgirl. Only part of the prejudiced 23% may be expected to express negative reactions when faced with a *fait accompli*. Even the few who do object to the accomplished fact are likely to do so only verbally rather than via the predicted extreme behavior of changing salesgirls or changing stores. Thus, my hypothesis is confirmed: *Employers who hire Negroes in public-contact positions generally experience no negative customer reactions; employers who have not hired Negroes in public-contact positions generally assume that their customers might react negatively.*

Chapter 6

Discrimination and Prejudice

The job ceiling is a mechanism of discrimination. We ordinarily assume that discriminatory behavior is caused by prejudiced attitudes. A prejudiced public is assumed by managers who recommend educating that public about fair employment. Pressure groups take it for granted that discriminating managers are prejudiced. Hostility toward Negroes is imputed by observers to those who fail to hire Negroes.

Discrimination is assumed to be caused by prejudice in the following quotation: "The decreasing discrimination as we go from South to North ... is apparently related to a weaker basic prejudice" (Myrdal, 1944). Noland and Bakke (1949) blame discrimination in New Haven factories on managerial prejudices about Negro abilities:

> No signs appeared over the employment offices of New Haven ... firms reading "Negroes need not apply." But for all practical purposes that sign was out for clerical applicants. ... Nine-tenths of [the employers] in New Haven had strong preferences against Negroes in clerical jobs. ... The chief qualifications established by employers for clerical workers ... [are] education, character, and personality traits. ... Rightly or wrongly, employers believe Negroes to be inferior to whites in these respects.

Maslow and Robinson generalize that "we may safely assume that discrimination is a result of prejudiced attitudes—that discrimination would not exist without prejudice."

Schermerhorn (1949), on the other hand, is uncertain about which is cause and which is effect. He suggests that discrimination may be practiced by persons who are not initially prejudiced.

> Theoretically, discrimination may be practiced without prejudice, as for example in the case of a newcomer into a community who joins the dominant group and acts in Rome "as the Romans do" without sharing the attitudes and feelings of the community but hesitates to break over the lines of discrimination for fear of coming into general disfavor. He may personally fail to share any of the group prejudices, at least to begin with. Gradual habituation to segregating others, however, will eventually have its inevitable effect, and the practices of the society

will come to have a normative value, so that the proper emotions and feelings are aroused when the folkways are violated.

But Schermerhorn's main approach is an interaction point of view. "The folkways of discrimination reinforce the stereotype of inferiority as applied to the minority and thus freeze minority members into an artificial occupational distribution." He relegates the question of whether prejudice or discrimination came first to the chicken-or-the-egg category.

> In the social analysis of prejudice and discrimination it becomes clear that neither can be given priority over the other. Both arise by a process of mutual interaction. There are some who believe that prejudice is more often the result of discrimination than discrimination the result of prejudice. This is a thesis that would be difficult to prove, although in areas of well-congealed discrimination and segregation it might be true (Schermerhorn, 1949).

All of the above interpretations assume that prejudice and discrimination are inseparably linked together, one way or another. Prejudice produces discrimination, or discrimination produces prejudice, or they are reciprocally interactive. However, there is a fourth alternative; either prejudiced attitudes or discriminatory behavior may exist apart from the other.

> Evidences from many sources point to the very loose relationship between opinions and attitudes (as expressed in interviews and questionnaires) and subsequent behavior with regard to the object of these opinions or attitudes (Williams, 1964).
>
> Attitudes and behavior need not always be congruent; particular situations can structure how most people behave in spite of the attitudes they may harbour (Pettigrew, 1966).
>
> ... An ever-accumulating body of research demonstrates that allegedly prejudiced persons act in a thoroughly egalitarian manner in situations where that is the socially prescribed mode of behavior ... (Kohn and Williams, 1956).

That prejudice need not govern actions is one of Saenger's findings for New York customers. The same thesis applies to Twin Cities employee responses as well. Wherever latent prejudice conflicts with the American Creed, the behavior invoked in a particular situation will depend on the circumstances. If an employee is controlled by forceful management leadership, or if a customer is faced with a *fait accompli*, a prejudiced attitude is not likely to produce discriminatory behavior. Under these circumstances, prejudice may continue to exist (as measured by an attitude questionnaire), but behavior is dominated by other values, such as social conformity.

Discrimination may also exist apart from prejudice. After reporting the disintegration of prejudice as a belief system, Myrdal (1944) ascribes the persistence of discrimination to cultural lag:

> The gradual destruction of the popular theory behind race prejudice is the most important of all social trends in the field of interracial relations.

The popular beliefs rationalizing caste in America are no longer intellectually respectable. . . . Everybody who has acquired a higher education knows that they are wrong.

The white man is thus in the process of losing confidence in the theory which gave reason and meaning to his way of life. And since he has not changed his way of life much, he is in a dilemma. This change is probably irreversible and cumulative. It is backed by the American Creed. The trend of psychology, education, anthropology, and social science is toward environmentalism in the explanation of group differences, which means that the racial beliefs which defended caste are being torn away. It also means, by implication, that the white majority group in power is accused of being the cause of the Negroes' deficiencies and unhappiness.

Several authors suggest that discrimination can be customary without being rooted in racial prejudice:

Employers in Chicago give a number of reasons for their failure to extend full job opportunity to Negroes. A few employers (these seem to be a minority) have stereotyped conceptions of what the Negro can and cannot do. A larger number do not question the Negro's capacity, but still feel that he should permanently occupy a subordinate place in the economic life of the society. Most employers, however, do not seem to have any clearcut, articulate convictions on the matter one way or another. They are simply hesitant to make innovations that might curtail production, cause trouble in the plant, or otherwise jeopardize their profits or prestige. Under normal conditions the hold of custom is heavy everywhere (Drake and Cayton, 1945).

Custom is similarly emphasized in Dean and Rosen's *Manual of Intergroup Relations* (1955):

An important mechanism for the perpetuation of segregated situations and discriminatory practices appears to be the relatively unquestioning acceptance by people in a community of the intergroup relations practices instituted by earlier customs or policy decisions and passed along as "the way we do things here."

Managerial Attitudes toward Negroes

The northern job ceiling appears to be a case of discrimination without prejudice. Only a minority of the Twin Cities managers expressed negative opinions about Negro abilities; only 30% predicted unsatisfactory Negro sales work (Table 3-1) and even fewer (4%) unsatisfactory clerical work (Table 3-3). Moreover, managers seldom based pessimistic predictions on stereotypes of inherent inability (Table 3-2).

Few managers ascribed inborn deficiencies to Negroes. The biological dogmas of racism were seldom expressed.[1] The closest resemblance to

---

[1] That prejudice remains unexpressed does not, of course, guarantee its absence. Arnold Rose points out, "Just because the employers don't express racism doesn't

prejudice was a St. Paul manager's reference to the "fancy cars and loud clothes" of local Negroes. But even these "Negro characteristics" were blamed on the present group of local Negroes rather than on defective germ plasm.

As in Chicago, it was somewhat more common to encounter among Twin Cities managers a belief that Negroes should establish a separate but equal society. One personnel manager suggested to the Urban League that "the colored should have their own department store, theater, etc., in the Negro district." Variations of a "they-have-their-place" philosophy were expressed by three other managers, one a recent migrant from Alabama. Only these four out of the 53 respondents expressed a segregationist philosophy. A nationwide survey in 1963 found northern white proprietors and managers less segregationist in attitude than any other occupational group except professionals (Sheatsley, 1966).

Many managers emphasized the social origin of current Negro limitations. One used the common local environment of Negroes and whites as an argument for equal ability: "They go to the same high schools. I haven't met any such, but if I had to find a Negro comptometer operator, I assume I could." Nevertheless, others blamed the inadequate training of Negroes on lack of access to facilities. One manager spoke of "handicaps in family background." Another ascribed Negro touchiness to previous discrimination. "The Negro race has been the underdog," said a third. Many of the managers emphasized differences in education and vocational training. One blamed the concentration of Negroes in janitorial work on "educational limitations." An owner-manager blamed the job ceiling in general on the "lack of training and education of Negroes." "If," said a personnel secretary, "they were given the same opportunities, they would be O.K., but they have usually been handicapped in getting training and education." However, a manager who had just arrived from Arkansas was so impressed by the school training available to Minnesota Negroes that he predicted clerical work as good as the average white stenographer's. "Here," he explained, "there are good schools which the Negroes can attend, in contrast with the situation in the South."

mean they don't have it. The employers are good at public relations, at covering up their private attitudes. But racism is a deep-lying element in our culture. Practically all whites have it in some form or other."

However, many hours of listening to the managers in a permissive atmosphere of confidence and neutrality failed to yield the expected clues to prejudice. If deprecatory attitudes did exist at a deeper level, projective techniques would have been necessary to reach them. The interview method for this study yielded no empirical evidence for calling more than a small minority of the managers prejudiced.

There is a significant difference between the verbalizations of the Twin Cities retail managers and those of New Haven industrial managers interviewed by Bakke. Whereas the latter "frequently" exhibited traditional stereotypes, only one-tenth of the Twin Cities managers did. Whether this difference at the verbal level indicates a corresponding difference in attitudes could be reliably determined only by more elaborate research methods.

After reading the interview schedules, Theodore Caplow observed that, to his surprise, "the responses of the managers are highly sociological in that they locate the problem in group responses and not in the Negro himself. This is a sophisticated point of view." Whether explaining why Twin Cities Negroes were as good as whites, or why the Negroes were not so good, the above managers agreed that the conditions under which the Negroes live are responsible for their disabilities.

Other managers rejected even sociological generalizations. Numbering almost half the total, 24 respondents rebelled when asked to evaluate the ability of the average Negro. To them there is no such thing as a typical Negro. "It's the individual, not the race," protested 11 managers. Eight asserted that there are "some good, some bad in every race." "There are all kinds of Negroes," said one. These attitudes are responsible for the large number of contingent predictions.

Similar emphasis on the importance of individual differences was encountered by the National Industrial Conference Board in the racial attitudes of officials of more than 100 companies: "It is interesting to find that many employers characterized the problem as 'distinctly individual rather than group'" (O'Connor, 1941). This approach is poles apart from thinking in terms of stereotypes, which "obscure individual differences entirely, and the person as person becomes a case in the category, a replaceable unit indifferently as good or as bad as any other" (Schermerhorn, 1949).

Our Twin Cities managers, as a rule, avoided broad generalizations. For those managers who did not generalize, individual Negroes were not members of a group so much as individual human beings with differing talents and personalities. This attitude makes fair-employment practices possible once other barriers are removed. The managers' own attitudes toward Negroes were seldom one of those barriers.

Finally, four managers emphasized not simply that Twin Cities Negroes had received the same training as whites, but that there is "no difference between white and Negro." Negroes are not inherently inferior but are "just as intelligent as whites." Some managers were so carried away by enthusiasm for equality that, ignoring the impact of discrimination on the minority group, they went considerably further than a sociologist would. They illustrated in extreme form the nonstereotyped thinking so common in the managers' attitudes toward Negroes.

"We Are Not Prejudiced, But . . ."

We have seen how rarely expressions of prejudice were encountered among the store managers. Indeed, they were anxious to avoid being considered prejudiced. They eagerly attested their belief in fair employment and protested any suggestion that their store policies conflicted with that ideal.

Whereas in New Haven, Noland and Bakke found a compulsion to apologize for discrimination in employment by devaluing Negro abilities, the Twin Cities managers seemed to be under a different sort of compulsion—to convince themselves and others that what appeared to be discrimination was not that at all. The old racial stereotypes as well as prejudice were taboo. Instead of using prejudice to justify discrimination, the managers argued that they did not discriminate.

In order to prove nondiscrimination, managers often redefined what discrimination "really means." As long as discrimination is not measured by such undodgeable criteria as quotas at every job level, managers could avoid obvious discrimination. To distinguish naïveté from deceit is not our concern. What is noteworthy is how often the respondents reacted defensively when asked presumably objective questions under the necessity to justify their own official practice.

In most cases, the managers felt they had worked out satisfactory solutions to their dilemma. But the resulting juxtaposition of diverse statements, or of statements and behavior, makes those solutions seem paradoxical to the outsider. I have highlighted the contradictions by placing in parallel columns the protestations of innocence and the evidence of discriminatory behavior. My own remarks are in parentheses.

Protestation	*Prejudice*
We have no preference as to race . . .	. . . in dishwashing or stockroom.
We are quite as willing to hire Negroes as whites . . .	. . . there. (No Negroes now. Formerly had some Negro janitors.)
I'm not the least bit prejudiced.	They have their place.
We can get along together well.	I prefer segregated jobs for them.
It works well and gives the company good standing . . .	. . . to hire nothing but Negroes for janitors.
I'm not opposed to Negroes.	But I am afraid of their monopolizing jobs if we give them a chance.
Everything will be O.K. . . .	. . . if they will only stay in their places.
Negroes should have a chance to prove themselves. It's too bad some companies do discriminate.	But a company ought to be able to hire whom they wish to.
We make no discrimination on any applicants. We hire on the basis of ability only.	(No Negroes among 800 office workers.)

We don't discriminate here; we have a happy relationship with colored people.

We believe in real equality of opportunity, in treating people as individuals.

Mr. ———— (store president) has always made quite a point of fairness and courtesy in treating Negro job applicants.

Employees are happy here.

This is a liberal company. The owner has no objection whatever to the employment of a colored person . . .

We welcome Negroes as customers and give them good treatment here. I've always gotten along well with Negroes.

I personally wouldn't mind light-skinned Negroes in the office . . .

I'm not opposed to Negroes. I would take those who applied if they were qualified . . .

I'm pretty broad-minded myself.

The intelligent Negro knows his place. (All Negro janitors in seven chain stores.)

(Lily-white office force of 125. Sales staff of 225. One Negro in shoe-repair department.)

Neither Negro sales nor clerical workers are being considered.

Problems in a store like this are different from larger stores. (275 employees, no union, no Negroes.)

. . . in the warehouse or for janitorial and cleaning work, but of course he would not want one on the sales or office staff.

But they are happier with their own people. Why give them jobs they don't want? It will only lead to intermarriage, and everyone objects to that. (Southerner.)

. . . but the employees might object.

. . . but none ever applied. (Whitney Young reported that he had offered to send over qualified applicants but had been turned down.) This is a racial survey. (Angry objection.)

But I wouldn't ever hire a Negro as long as I could get a white. I don't want to ask for trouble. (With the union.)

The left-hand column gives repeated evidence of the taboo on prejudice and the corresponding desire to make a liberal impression. "Caste may exist," says Myrdal, "but it cannot be recognized. Instead, the stamp of public disapproval is set upon it. . . . " In Myrdal's analysis (1944), the word "public" is particularly important since Americans behave differently in their public and private capacities.

There is plenty of discrimination in the North. But it is—or rather its rationalization is—kept hidden. We can, in the North, witness the legislators' obedience to the American Creed when they solemnly pass laws and regulations to condemn and punish such acts of discrimination which, as a matter of routine, are committed daily by the great majority of the white citizens and by the legislators themselves.

Myrdal's attempt to explain the paradoxes of the North is similar to Noland and Bakke's conflict analysis. When the managers emphasize their acceptance of the American Creed, they are speaking in the role of community leader. But where specific practice in their own stores is concerned, the managers shift to the role of enterprise leader.

Despite the fact that the Negro is ruthlessly discriminated against in private business, the civic ideal reasserts itself in the ambivalent struggle with discriminatory practices.

> ... The white Northerner is becoming prepared, *as a citizen,* to give the Negro his just opportunity. But apparently, as a private individual, he is less prepared to feel that he himself is the man to give the Negro a better chance: in his own occupation, trade union, office or workshop. ... The social paradox in the North is exactly this, that almost everybody is against discrimination in general but, at the same time, almost everybody practices discrimination in his own personal affairs (Myrdal, 1944).

The same conflict of roles characterized most of our store managers. They, too, opposed discrimination in general and rejected the principle of unequal treatment. Yet their stores almost unexceptionally practiced discrimination.

Of the four possible combinations of prejudice and discrimination, most managers were *unprejudiced discriminators* (Merton, 1949a). A large minority were *unprejudiced nondiscriminators.* This group included the pioneering managers who had voluntarily hired the first Negro office workers and most of those who had succumbed to pressure and hired the first Negro salesgirls in spite of fears about repercussions from white employees and customers. A smaller minority were *prejudiced discriminators,* who verbalized their prejudice (sometimes without realizing that they were doing so) and discriminated in employment (often, again, without full awareness or conscious intent). Rarest of all were *prejudiced nondiscriminators,* although one personnel manager who grudgingly hired Negro salesgirls under the combined pressure of his boss and the Urban League clearly fell in this category. With increased pressure from outside groups, others might shift from prejudiced and unprejudiced discrimination to prejudiced or unprejudiced nondiscrimination.

Discrimination without Prejudice

Among the Twin Cities managers, prejudice was rare. But discrimination in employment persisted, even though that discrimination was outlawed in one city and considered immoral in both. The postwar breakthroughs had scarcely changed the overall pattern.

How can a practice so widely condemned be so firmly entrenched? A Marxian analyst might contend that the job ceiling is a bourgeois stratagem for exploiting either the workers in general (divide and conquer) or the Negroes in particular (through discriminatory wage scales). Presumably there were too few Negroes in the Twin Cities to make a divide-and-conquer strategy relevant. On the other hand, the job ceiling certainly created a reserve of cheap labor, so that managers always knew where to turn when they needed another janitor. By cutting Negroes off from alternative job opportunities, the ceiling decreased their bargaining potential and drove down the wages they could command.

However, janitorial positions were so few and so unimportant in the retail employment structure that the managers were unlikely to be motivated either consciously or unconsciously by any urge to cut costs or guarantee a labor supply in this way.

Moreover, the difference between being a cleaning lady and being a salesgirl is not primarily a matter of money. Salesgirls, too, are notoriously ill paid. But to be a salesgirl is to have a much better job in terms of prestige and working conditions. Selling is a cleaner job, a literally white-collar job. Hence the ceiling discriminated more socially than economically. And economic analysis hardly explains social discrimination.

A functionalist might assert that the sheer existence of the job ceiling proves that it meets a need, or functional requirement, of the retail store as a social system. To the average manager, this argument sounds plausible. The job ceiling is supposedly necessary for maintaining the carefully built network of employee and customer relationships. However, employer images of employee and customer attitudes do not correspond with employee and customer behavioral responses to Negro breakthroughs. Hence, the ceiling is at best pseudo-functional.

Two theories about the job ceiling must be rejected. What alternative explanations emerge from the Twin Cities data?

No Applications

In the first place, the ceiling was self-perpetuating. Many managers never encountered Negro applicants for sales or clerical jobs, despite the fact that an Urban League survey of St. Paul janitors and porters showed that one in four was capable of skilled work. If a store has never hired Negroes for skilled work, the average Negro assumes that the store never will. The ceiling is not enforced by rejecting Negroes; rather, it discourages Negroes from applying to begin with. Myrdal (1944) describes this process.

> If an establishment is a "white shop," Negroes generally know this. Few of them ever try to get in—and those few who make the attempt can tell the rest of the Negro job-seekers about how futile it has been. In such cases Negroes are excluded with a minimum of effort on the part of ... employers. ... Most white people never think of the fact that there is a definite policy to keep the Negro out. The "white shop" is part of the tradition and just seems "natural." The issue is not faced. The color bar, although as real as it can be, is almost invisible.

Few employers go out of their way to seek Negro skilled employees, even for the sake of token employment. Hence, as long as Negroes assume that retail jobs are unavailable, the situation remains unchanged.

Unawareness

One corollary of the ease with which the job ceiling operates is widespread ignorance of the seriousness of job discrimination in the Twin Cities. The small proportion of Negroes in the local population facilitates this ignorance. Social segregation between whites and Negroes of similar social status, and between managers and workers generally, blocks communication of Negro grievances to whites who are in a position to make amends.

White soldiers in World War II were similarly unaware of Negro feelings. Over half of the northern soldiers, and two-thirds of the Southerners, thought most Negroes were satisfied with their position in American society.

Only a tenth of the Southerners and a seventh of the Northerners said "most are dissatisfied." . . . This apparent lack of awareness on the part of whites of attitudes which are rather widespread in the Negro group tends, in part, to result from cultural isolation which minimizes personal contacts between the races and thereby reduces opportunities for whites to learn the thoughts and feelings of Negroes . . . [and also from] the tendency on the part of the Negroes to conceal their attitudes protectively from whites (Stouffer, 1949).

Given the assumption that Negroes are satisfied with their lot, it is natural —not malicious—to deduce that no change is needed. Almost two-thirds (64%) of Stouffer's white soldiers thought that the status of Negroes after the war should remain "about the same." Only 20% felt that Negroes should have "more rights and privileges," while the balance were split into undecided and more conservative fragments. Similarly, most Twin Cities managers had not heard of the dissatisfaction of local Negroes with their employment opportunities; those managers could say in all innocence, "There is no discrimination in Minnesota."

Part of the discrepancy lies in differing definitions of discrimination. The occasional advocates of segregation and the more frequent boasters about Negro janitors fell in this category. As long as a manager defined nondiscrimination as anything short of equality of opportunity throughout the employment hierarchy, he could be smugly proud of what was actually token employment or underemployment. Most managers had given little thought to the race problem. As a result, their definitions of discrimination were fuzzy.

Looking at the job ceiling from the standpoint of their individual stores, the managers failed to realize the magnitude of the problem on a city-wide scale. Although they preferred not to hire Negroes at unusual levels in their own establishments, these managers did not deliberately intend to consign skilled Negroes to unskilled jobs. Since no one employer controls all the jobs in a city, a manager can always hope that a Negro applicant will find the right job somewhere else. But when all managers pass Negroes on to the next prospective employer, the combined result is an insurmountable barrier.

A Negro lad in Minneapolis, Minnesota, had successfully prepared himself . . . to become an electrician. . . . He encountered difficulties in getting . . . employment, in spite of the best personal recommendations and in spite of assistance from the local Urban League. Most of the contractors declared that they themselves had nothing against engaging him. *They were not prejudiced*, they explained, but they had to abstain on account of occasional customers who were prejudiced.

I made some inquiries and found that most housewives I questioned did not mind. A few stated that they felt they rather wanted to have white workers around in the house. . . . They did not realize how their *slight and unmotivated* bias had the *cumulated effect* of closing employment opportunities to great numbers of Negro youths (Myrdal, 1944, emphasis added).

As long as individual employers (or employees or customers) regard the employment of Negroes from the perspective of one store at a time, the dimensions of the problem will not be visible. Within such limited horizons, each of these groups enforces the job ceiling without realizing the consequences.

Inertia

Ignorance is convenient; it upholds the status quo. Unchallenged by either the insistence of Negro applicants or by awareness of any discrepancy between ideals and practice, the pattern of lily-white sales and clerical staffs became entrenched with the years. Custom made change difficult, and the job ceiling acquired the force of convention and habit. For example, in one Twin Cities store, Negro applicants were automatically referred to a department where customer contact was not involved. In other stores it was taken for granted that Negro applicants wanted to be janitors. The job ceiling persisted because it had always been there.

Employee Risks

Even if the three factors of no applications, unawareness, and inertia suddenly disappeared, the job ceiling would not have collapsed. Their disappearance might have made the managers wish to achieve fair employment in their stores. But discrimination did not depend on the managers' attitudes toward Negroes. It resulted from the managers' assumptions about other white residents of the Twin Cities. Other people were perceived to be prejudiced, and that perception was the most stubborn obstacle to fair employment.

Imputing prejudice to others is not peculiar to managers.

When talking about the Negro problem, everybody ... is ... anxious to locate race prejudice outside himself. The impersonal "public opinion" or "community feelings" are held responsible. The whites practically never discuss the issue in terms of "I" or "we" but always in terms of "they," "people in the South," "people in this community," or "folks down here will not stand for ... " this or that. One can go around for weeks talking to white people in all walks of life and constantly hear about the wishes and beliefs of this collective being, yet seldom meeting a person who actually identifies himself with it. But he follows it (Myrdal, 1944).

In the Army, a majority of those advocating separate outfits for Negro and white soldiers argued from expediency. Only a few white soldiers expressed personal dislike of Negroes or believed in segregation in principle, but several times as many cited the prejudices of others to justify the status quo (Stouffer, 1949).

Nor were Twin Cities managers different from businesssmen elsewhere. In Chicago,

employers in general maintain that they are not responsible for discrimination against Negro labor—almost always they tend to assign responsibility for the policy to their employees ... (Drake and Cayton, 1945).

Each manager is officially the leader of an enterprise. Of the number of roles that each manager plays, the specific one that discourages Negro employment is the role of "risk reducer."

Faced with no certain future, these managers were interested in reducing the uncertainty at every possible point. Every barrier set up to the employment of certain types of workers was an exercise of this function. Every effort to obtain workers with qualities one could "count on" was an attempt to meet this responsibility and necessity intelligently. Employers insist they have no right to take risks when these can be reduced, as they can in the careful selection of workers. They are trustees for the stockholders' money when the firm is incorporated, and that function requires them to reduce risks whenever possible (Noland and Bakke, 1949).

Concerned with minimizing risks, three-fifths of the Twin Cities employers who had not yet employed Negroes at skilled levels predicted at least the possibility of unfavorable reactions from both their sales and clerical staffs. Over half of these managers were convinced that they would get negative repercussions, while the rest interpreted the situation as containing unpredictable risks for the store's closely knit team of employees.[2]

The trouble with the manager's image of his employees is not that he falsely assumes they are prejudiced but that he believes their prejudices

[2] ... This concern is a persistent one and applies to white workers who are atypical as well as to Negroes. The concern is merely raised to a superlative degree in relation to the hiring of Negroes" (Noland and Bakke, 1949).

will inevitably govern their reactions to Negro employees. He fails to see that employees are ambivalent enough in their own attitudes to make their behavior depend on their manager's leadership. Given an image of inevitable, or at least possible, dissension among his employees, the manager considers the job ceiling a necessary safeguard for his employee relations.

Customer Risks

The job ceiling for sales work is reinforced by the manager's image of his customers. Here the manager is even more pessimistic than about his employees since he has no authority over customers. While a troublesome employee might be replaced, "the customer is always right." As we have seen, only one-fourth of our managers felt confident of favorable customer reactions, whereas a much higher percentage predicted negative reactions, especially loss of customers to competitors (Table 5-1). In Chicago, too,

> employers often "pass the buck" (consciously or unconsciously) to the public, instead of, or as well as, to their employees: "Educate the public to accept Negroes in the better jobs and we'll hire them," they say. "We can't risk losing our customers" (Drake and Cayton, 1945).

These images of employee reaction and customer reaction survive because few managers hear about the favorable experience of their peers who have placed the first Negroes above the ceiling. Still fewer managers are willing to generalize from department stores to other types of stores. Few are even willing to generalize from experience with one type of employee to another type. As a result, the myths about recalcitrant employees and alienated customers continue to reinforce the managers' natural conservatism.

The Managerial Dilemma

Caught between conflicting roles, managers are in an awkward position. (1) All of them are *enterprise leaders*. In this role, their responsibility is to maximize profits and minimize losses. Change of any kind introduces unknown risks and threatens the status quo. The reaction of any businessman to unnecessary risks is to avoid them. To integrate the sales force of a store operating on a precarious margin and engaged in stiff competition for customers is to risk offending customers and demoralizing the existing staff. As enterprise leaders, managers of segregated stores stress their fears of these unknown risks as ample reason for upholding the status quo. To oppose the F.E.P.C. is another way of protecting the enterprise from the forced introduction of risks.

(2) On the other hand, most managers also conceive of themselves as *community leaders*. Their high social status gives them a perspective on

community problems and a sense of *noblesse oblige.* Their superior education helps them to understand the problems of other people and other races. As patriotic Americans, the managers believe in the American Creed. Hence, once confronted with the problems of any segment of the community, the managers cannot ignore them. Such men must accept fair employment as an objective, if not legislation as a method. They like to consider themselves liberal-minded and like to brag about their human-relations accomplishments once their own resistance to risks has been overcome.

(3) For some managers, there is a third role: *defender of minority rights.* For Jewish managers, this role is a normal part of one's conception of the self. Members of a minority themselves (with memories of Buchenwald all too fresh), they find it easy to empathize with the plight of the Negro and easy to be suspicious of W.A.S.P.s. In the Twin Cities, both sentiments made the F.E.P.C. appealing. Jewish managers wanted to spur Negro employment but at the same time to protect Jewish stores from unfair competition by presumably prejudiced Gentile stores. W.A.S.P. customers were similarly deemed likely to act unfairly and desert pioneering stores for still-segregated competitors.

The Jewish managers' consciousness of their own minority status made them both more eager to aid Negroes and more fearful of the risks involved. Just because a man was Jewish, therefore, did not mean he would necessarily pioneer in race relations. Sometimes the risk-reducing role won out.

Most managers, Jewish or not, felt the strain of role conflict. Managers who opposed the F.E.P.C. on risk-reducing grounds felt obliged to protect themselves from accusations of selfishness by invoking community-oriented arguments. Inner conflict over discriminatory employment policies was minimized by redefining discriminatory behavior as nondiscriminatory or by paying lip service to democratic ideals and simply failing to apply those ideals to overt behavior.

Left to themselves, most managers' inner conflict created so much ambivalence that they were locked in an indifferent equilibrium, which perpetuated the status quo. Despite the fact that pioneering breakthroughs had occurred elsewhere in their metropolis, most inexperienced managers were ignorant of the experience of their peers. Hence, the inexperienced managers' predictions of customer and employee reactions could not be demythologized. As far as those managers were concerned, neither customers nor employees could be trusted to swallow change.

Nevertheless, the key to customer and employee response lay in the managers' own hands. The crucial concept was *definition of the situation.* Managers were not the only ones caught in role conflict. Ordinary people, too, were torn between fears of the untried and hopes for democracy. They, too, were in a state of indifferent equilibrium. Hence, their response to controversial innovations would depend on the psychological definition that they gave the situation. So great was the ambivalence of other people that their definition could easily be influenced by managerial propaganda. Announcement of reasons for adopting a fair-employment policy is especially likely to influence employee behavior in small stores with short communication lines. Threats of punishment ("conform or else") are likely to suppress any predispositions to negative reactions by employees. Actually, most employees and even more customers are too spontaneously conformist to challenge managerial action once it is accomplished. The *fait accompli* is a powerful weapon. Whether people like change or not, few of them are brave enough to mount a counterrevolution.

Hence, managers who thought they were caught in a role conflict could resolve it by using their role of enterprise leader to achieve their community aspirations. To break out of the dilemma, the managers needed to know how false their fears were and how great their powers.

Part 2

The Dynamics of Change

With so many factors operating to preserve the job ceiling, what were the potentials for change? The chief resource within the stores themselves lay in certain attitudes of the managers (Chapter 7). Their commitment to the American Creed and their pride in pioneering once they had been persuaded to do so could furnish power for revising institutionalized practices.

But the managers were wearing blinders. The managers seldom recognized the inconsistencies in their own behavior. They did not realize that their underemployment and even their token employment of Negroes were discriminatory. The managers were unaware of the consequences of their practices for the Negro community at large.

To charge discrimination effectively is a delicate matter. The lesson is likely to be learned best if it is self-taught. Removing blinders was only part of the job to be done, only a means that might increase the desire for change. Indeed, this approach can fail.

> . . . Inconsistency is a charge that does not bite deep. . . . Most men seem to get along on some kind of compromise with their creeds, and they are adept enough at makeshift adjustments in the ordinary business of living. It is well to expose their rationalizations but nevertheless they have great capacity for finding new ones. They may have some uneasiness on this score, but often it is not potent enough to make them change their ways. Furthermore, it by no means follows that this uneasiness will of itself make for greater tolerance and be a stage on the road to understanding. Guilt feelings are uncomfortable and they may be got rid of by a harder and blinder defensiveness, supported by new justifications, so that the spirit of discrimination is not diminished but rather intensified (MacIver, 1948).

In order for a heightened sense of guilt to issue in constructive action, the condition of pluralistic ignorance must be broken through. Managerial images of inevitable damage to customer and employee relations must be shattered by knowledge of favorable experience. Moreover, the managers needed, via precise instructions, reassurance in how to minimize and control negative employee reactions.

But it is not enough for managers to be motivated and instructed. This study suggests that constant pressure from concerned agencies is necessary to persuade managers to take the trouble of embarking on new ventures. And when new steps are taken, managerial boldness might be enhanced if the community devised ways of acknowledging the leadership exerted by pioneering managers.

The weakest spot in the Twin Cities job ceiling related to clerical employment. There the customer phobia does not operate. Two-thirds of the managers believed that local Negro girls could be found who would be competent stenographers. And more than half foresaw either favorable reactions or no reaction from white office workers.[1]

But at both sales and clerical levels, some managers were prepared to move ahead. And if the agencies concerned with fair employment conduct a vigorous long-term campaign, more Negroes could break through the job ceiling (Chapters 8–10).

---

[1]Of the four stores employing Negroes in clerical capacities, only one also had Negro salesgirls. Of the three having Negro stenographers but not salesgirls, two employed chiefly salesmen rather than saleswomen (the barriers were higher to employment of Negro men in skilled jobs), and the third was an "exclusive" store with a highly trained sales staff. In specialized stores the training and experience necessary for clerical jobs is less extensive and more accessible to Negroes than that required for sales jobs.

Chapter 7

Managerial Readiness for Employment Breakthroughs

It would be wrong to assume that all employment breakthroughs in the North occur in spite of the personnel managers. They do fear employee and customer repercussions, but the managers also believe in the American Creed. Once they have integrated their sales or clerical staff, they are proud of their achievement. Some managers, despite their fears, even take the initiative in employing Negroes where none has ever worked before. It would be unfair to the managers—and bitterly resented by them—to give all the credit for employment breakthroughs to outside pressures.

Managerial Liberalism

Three of every five managers employing Negro salesgirls and three of the four with Negro office workers named their own liberalism as at least one of the factors responsible for their new company policy. Nor were those who had never hired Negroes above the ceiling necessarily conservative in their racial attitudes. Opening doors to Negroes was actively being considered by half the managers for their sales forces and by more than a third for their office staffs. Both groups of managers credited their own liberalism as a major motive (27% for potential sales breakthroughs and 13% for clerical work).

Sometimes it was the top executive of a store who was interested in hiring Negroes, but other times it was a lower official. Several department foremen or buyers in charge of departments had employed, or were interested in employing, Negroes above the ceiling. In these cases, top management was usually willing to let the subordinate experiment in his own department, even though there might be no plan to extend the policy throughout the store. In the first three Minneapolis stores that employed Negro office workers, the individuals responsible were an owner-manager, a personnel director, and a department head. These stores illustrate the variety of levels in the management hierarchy where initiative may be taken. Where top management took a liberal position, that view was customarily communicated to the personnel manager. But other cases prove that the top executive need not be convinced of the desirability of employing Negroes in order for his store to begin doing so.

If managerial liberalism were the only factor involved in employment breakthroughs, they would have occurred long before World War II. But liberalism does not operate in a social vacuum; liberalism is triggered by changes in the environment. One personnel manager indicated that his boss had complied with the F.E.P.C. from "a sense of responsibility" but would probably not have taken any initiative without the law. A St. Paul personnel manager reported that her store manager had been "ready to go along" with a state F.E.P.C. law by employing Negro salesgirls in his store. In both stores, management "initiative" consisted of responding positively to outside pressure.

The manager who hazarded the first Minneapolis sales experiment recognized that the Urban League, the Joint Committee for Employment Opportunity, and the F.E.P.C. had all played a part in the company's decision. Management had seen the trend toward equal employment opportunity: "We knew it was coming." However, she reserved for management much of the credit for the decision. "We had been thinking about it," she said. With obvious pride, she dismissed the idea that her store was just jumping on a department-store bandwagon. "We did it first. We would have done it anyway, whether or not ————'s did."

Regardless of the fact that the first impulse for hiring Negroes may come from outside groups, the final decision is made by management itself. Managers felt they could have said no if they had wanted to. When they said yes (even after initial hostility), the managers took both the responsibility and the credit for the decision and thus viewed it as their own. In the Twin Cities, the employment of Negroes above the job ceiling could easily have been defined as a humanitarian gesture. As a result, many managers, in retrospect, bragged about their role in the decision to hire Negroes in new jobs.

Suggestive of the memory changes that can result from this need for self-congratulation is a comparison of the breakthrough dates reported by Minneapolis personnel directors with the presumably accurate dates listed in a bulletin of the Joint Committee for Employment Opportunity. Two of the seven Minneapolis respondents thought their stores had been using Negro salesgirls approximately eight months longer than the bulletin reports. This exaggeration of one's own benevolence is typical of the managers' desire to make the best of what did not necessarily start out to be desirable.

Managers vary greatly in their readiness to take initiative. Many are strongly liberal. Conspicuous among these was a personnel manager whose store was the only one actively considering a Negro salesman. This respondent concluded the interview by asking, "How does this compare with other stores?" When told that his views were considerably more liberal than average, he commented, "Good. That's the way we want to be."

Of the Twin Cities respondents, 20 were considering employing Negroes in sales positions, and almost as many (17) were considering the possibility of hiring Negro clerical workers. Several managers indicated that they had pretty much decided to create openings for the right persons, should they come along. One personnel director's boss had already told him to consider each Negro applicant on his own merits. Another personnel manager, pointing to the owner's respectable (German-Irish) ethnic stock, illustrated the owner's "tolerant attitude for many years" by his continuing employment of "some Jews, Catholics, *et al.* and by the fact that the store during the war had some Nisei help and I had had a Negro on part-time sales in the past." In fact, this manager stated explicitly that the store had had a "longtime readiness to hire qualified Negroes" for both sales and clerical work.

Managerial readiness to employ Negroes in new positions had not yet been fully exploited in 1949. Because of the small size of both the Negro labor force and the pressure organizations, some managers had hardly been touched by the drive for integration.

Seven managers said they were willing to hire Negroes in sales and clerical positions but had never encountered qualified applicants. Some of these managers had never received even an unqualified applicant for a breakthrough job. Another store in the sample had been primed for employing Negroes in new positions by the fact that whites of the right quality seemed unavailable.[1] Such comments indicate that much of the room for expanding Negro job opportunities in the Twin Cities lay not in persuading managers that fair employment is desirable but in spreading the flow of Negro applicants to more stores.

Correspondingly, three respondents employing Negro salesgirls and another with Negro stenographers had been motivated at least in part by the simple fact that competent Negroes applied when vacancies existed. "They looked clean, neat, and experienced; we had a vacancy, so we hired them." These few cases mark the beginnings of an attitude that will prevail throughout the Twin Cities when the job ceiling is gone and forgotten.

Only two respondents (both in St. Paul) confessed to having rejected qualified applicants. One of these managers had received several qualified applicants for clerical work. The other had investigated the experience records of Negro applicants for sales work but hesitated to hire any because they were unfamiliar (inevitably) with the specialized merchandise of the store. However, receiving these qualified applicants nudged both managers toward eventually trying Negroes in higher positions.

---

[1]The smaller the proportion of Negroes in the community, the lower the probability that management will exhaust the supply of qualified whites and be forced to turn to the Negro labor pool. Conversely, in cities with a large Negro labor supply and a proportionately smaller supply of whites, Negro breakthroughs are more often motivated by labor shortages.

For other stores, practical considerations prompted the eventual hiring of Negroes. One store was looking for a Negro salesgirl in the hope that hiring one would increase the number of Negro customers. In a second, the Negro trade was already large ("we're a middle-class store, not like the exclusive shops"), and it seemed appropriate that Negroes should be represented on the sales staff, too.

Jewish versus Gentile Stores

A major source of managerial liberalism in Twin Cities stores was the Jewish ethnic identity of many managers. Jewish managers were almost always human-relations conscious, even when they were not liberal in their store policies or their political attitudes.

For example, one manager said that, because he was Jewish, he had to support the F.E.P.C., while a second confessed that his opposition to the practice (not the principle) of F.E.P.C. came in spite of his Jewishness. One personnel manager, himself a Gentile, pointed to the employment pattern of his chain as evidence of the liberality of the owners: "This chain is owned by two Jews and has a number of Jews in the organization. Therefore they have a high degree of tolerance. I think the home office has Negroes in it." A store manager was not sure how his customers would react to a Negro salesgirl, but he said, "If any customers objected, I'd say, 'To hell with them.' You see I'm Jewish and have had a taste of discrimination myself." These unsolicited references to Jewish minority status spurred me to examine the influence of this factor in the Twin Cities generally.

Rather than dividing the respondents by their personal affiliation (with no accurate information to go on), I decided to categorize the *stores* as Jewish or Gentile.[2] The sample split into 22 Jewish stores and 28 Gentile stores. In the Minneapolis sample, Gentiles predominated (18 to 11), while in the St. Paul group, Jews did (11 to 10). Jews were concentrated in furniture and clothing stores. In furniture stores, the ratio of Jews to Gentiles was 6 to 2 and in clothing, 11 to 4. The highly competitive field of women's clothing stores broke sharply into exclusive shops and moderately priced chain stores. All but one of the former were Gentile (three of the four), whereas all five chains were Jewish. By contrast, of the six drug, hardware, and stationery specialty stores, only one, a drug system, was Jewish. Low-priced variety stores were controlled by Gentiles by 3 to 1, and only three of the 13 department stores were Jewish. The four largest department stores in each city (which were also the four largest stores of any type) were Gentile.

[2]This division was made by Samuel L. Scheiner, of the Minnesota Jewish Council. That this division did not yield pure categories is obvious from the above example of the Gentile personnel manager who worked for a Jewish company.

From this breakdown, it is apparent that Jewish stores were of types that seldom employed Negroes above the ceiling. Their stores were small, competitive, chain outlets, which we have previously analyzed as operating on so precarious a margin that risk-taking is especially dangerous. Hence, there is little point in attempting to measure the effect of Jewish management by seeing which stores gave way to the pressure to employ Negro salesgirls. The big Gentile department stores could afford to take the presumed risks in ways the Jewish clothing stores could not.

At the semiskilled "other service" level, however, a fair comparison may be made between Jewish and Gentile employment policies, for at this level the type of store makes less difference. Jewish stores hired a larger proportion of Negroes in semiskilled jobs (7%, as compared to 4% of the Gentile stores' employees). The discrepancy would be even greater but for the fact that two Gentile stores employed over half of all the semiskilled Negroes in the entire 28 non-Jewish stores. Over half (54%) of the Gentile stores employed no Negroes whatsoever in "other service" capacities, in comparison to less than a fourth (23%) of the Jewish stores. In other words, where store conditions were roughly the same, managers of Gentile stores were twice as likely to have a lily-white labor force.

Jewish and Gentile managers differed little in their predictions about quality of Negro sales work. However, somewhat more Jewish managers expected satisfactory work, whereas Gentile managers were more often doubtful (prediction: "mixed").

In predicting the reaction of their office employees to Negro colleagues, managers of Jewish stores clustered at the neutral and ambivalent points of "no reaction," "unpredictable," and "it depends on the individual." Managers of Gentile stores were more divided. More of this group expected a favorable reaction, but the modal prediction was still unfavorable. Thus more managers of Jewish stores expected Negro employees to be accepted in the same fashion as new white office workers.

Predictions of customer reactions vary considerably between the two cities. In St. Paul, both Jewish and Gentile groups show a normal distribution of predictions, with the majority in the middle. In Minneapolis, however, respondents from Jewish stores were universally pessimistic. Some respondents from Gentile stores made similar predictions, but many felt neutral, and a few were even optimistic.

To summarize these three tests, the managers in Jewish stores were slightly more matter-of-fact about the response of their office staffs to the introduction of a Negro stenographer. But in Minneapolis, the Jewish managers' predictions of customer response were characterized by an unmitigated pessimism not shared by their Gentile counterparts. Perhaps Minneapolis Jewish managers perceived their predominantly Gentile customers as an out group characterized by prejudices that they themselves did not hold. These managers were usually not prejudiced toward Negroes but assumed that others (both employees and customers) would be. Since Jewish managers were more sympathetic to the employment of Negroes and since they managed smaller stores, the previous discussion of the role of leadership in the employee situation reveals why those managers could be confident of their ability to minimize the reaction of their office workers. But over customers, no manager has any control. This inability to control customer reactions creates a feeling of hopelessness, which is exaggerated by perceiving customers as bigoted Gentiles.

In attitudes toward the F.E.P.C., a Jewish propensity toward support is to be expected because the F.E.P.C. benefits Jews as well as Negroes. In Minneapolis, the Jewish stores' respondents applauded the F.E.P.C. by 6 to 3, whereas Gentile managers gave the law only a 7 to 6 edge. In St. Paul, sentiment in favor of the F.E.P.C. was less common; the Jewish stores' managers deadlocked 4 to 4, whereas the Gentile group were against the law by 4 to 2. In both cities, managers of Gentile stores more often gave the noncommittal "neutral" and "do not know" responses. However, the only two stores with policies of "no comment" on political issues were both Jewish owned and controlled.

In summary, the managers of Jewish stores were consistently more liberal. When the differentiating variable of type of store is held constant, Jewish stores are more liberal in employing Negroes, in appraising Negro ability, and in predicting employee reaction. Along with this attitude goes a greater tendency to support the F.E.P.C.[3] Forebodings of unpleasant customer reactions may likewise be a product of personal familiarity with discrimination. In view of these findings, Jewish liberalism becomes one of the significant factors that predispose managers to respond positively to pressure groups working to raise the Negro job ceiling.[4]

Established versus New Stores

A store's age may produce freedom of managerial action. If the executive of an old firm is prejudiced, old ways might be deeply entrenched. But if he is liberally inclined, a loyal following of customers attached to the store's good name might provide freedom to initiate new policies. Having fought the competitive battle and won, old stores need not be so cautious about unusual ventures as marginal new enterprises.

E. William Noland suggests:

The willingness of individual employers to hire Negroes in small firms seems to be a function of security, which, in turn, is a function of the

[3]Lenski (1954) finds status discrepancies between high income and low social esteem a source of political liberalism for American Jews.

[4]A nationwide survey in 1963 found Jews substantially more favorable toward integration in general than either Catholics or Protestants (Sheatsley, 1966).

age of the firm and the perspicacity of management. Where a company has many long-term employees with whom it has maintained good rapport, there is likely to be the greatest willingness to take risks (personal comment).

Holding Jewishness and type of store constant, I analyzed with respect to age two groups of stores—ten Jewish clothing stores and 13 Gentile department stores. Comparison of the old and new halves of these groups revealed few significant differences. Managers of older stores made almost exactly the same predictions of customer response and of sales and clerical employee responses as managers of newer stores did.

Managers of the five new Jewish clothing stores founded since 1933 tended toward extremes of optimism and pessimism, whereas those connected with stores founded prior to 1922 (there were none in between) made moderate predictions of "no reaction" from any source.

Comparison of the old (pre-World War I) and the new Gentile department stores is complicated by the fact that all seven of the former were employing Negro salesgirls, whereas none of the latter had done so up to August 1949. (The larger size and downtown location of the older stores account for most of this liberal employment pattern.) The sales employee and customer predictions of the inexperienced post-World War I stores likewise tended to fan out in both directions in comparison to the predictions of the experienced stores. This relationship fits our earlier discovery of the moderating effect of practical experience with Negroes.

Experience may be held constant by comparing six old and six new department stores; none of these stores had any Negro stenographers. Four old stores saw no risk from their white office workers, but five new ones predicted trouble. Similarly, seven of eight respondents from old department stores favored or were neutral toward a local F.E.P.C., but four of the six from new stores opposed such laws.

What do these observations prove about the effects of a store's age? Insofar as managers of newer stores made a wider range of predictions, this analysis throws doubt on our supposition that those managers would be more cautious. The greater liberality of officials of older department stores on some topics (clerical employee reaction and the F.E.P.C.) may reflect the age of the store. However, these analyses cannot be considered as more than exploratory in value.

Large versus Small Stores

The manager of a small store should feel able to control his employees. Analysis of predictions of employee reaction by size of store discloses such a relationship in the Twin Cities. In order to contrast predictions of employee reaction, respondents were grouped into a minority who saw no risk whatever, and thus predicted favorable reactions or no reaction, and a larger group who forsaw a considerable range of risks from their employees. For both sales and clerical staffs, the median stores that saw no risk were smaller than those worried about negative employee reactions (see Table 7-1).

Table 7-1

Median Number of Employees by Managers' Predictions of White Employees' Reaction to Negro Sales and Clerical Workers

	MEDIAN NUMBER OF EMPLOYEES BY CITY & PREDICTED REACTION			
	MINNEAPOLIS		ST. PAUL	
JOB CATEGORY	NO RISK	RISKY	NO RISK	RISKY
Sales	95	150	62	117
Clerical	95	157	100	156

Note: Two southern-born managers were excluded from this tabulation since their uniquely extreme predictions probably resulted from their cultural background rather than from their stores' size and since their predictions presumably would have held constant no matter what the size of store.

Although on the whole the Twin Cities managers were rather liberal, such views were accentuated by certain personal and situational factors. Jewish managers were more ideologically committed to integration. Managers of smaller stores felt more confident of their hold over their employees, and managers of stores with long-established reputations felt more confident of their hold over their customers. Such variations suggest the weak points in the ceiling where outside pressures are most likely to produce new openings.

Chapter 8

The Breakthrough Pressure Groups

The first Negro office girls were indebted to managerial initiative, but the first salesgirls owed their jobs to outside pressure. Liberal attitudes alone are seldom enough to produce social change. Liberalism needs to be triggered by outside forces if it is to be put into practice. Moreover, it is sometimes an after-the-fact rationalization of changes that are entirely the result of external pressures. Erstwhile conservatives may resist change, succumb to pressures, and then boast of their contribution to social progress. In either case, the role of pressure groups is to present the case for change so forcefully that the establishment must yield, whether willingly or grudgingly.

In the Twin Cities in 1949, four organizations were actively promoting integrated employment. The oldest was the Urban League, organized separately in each city and for years engaged in attempting to solve the practical problems of individual Negroes, case by case. Three new organizations were active in Minneapolis alone. Like other cities around the nation, Minneapolis needed a "Community Self-Survey of Human Relations" to discover and document local patterns of discrimination. A one-shot affair, the Self-Survey was designed to stir the public conscience and initiate moves toward equal opportunity. At the same time, a Joint Committee for Employment Opportunity was formed to spur the postwar drive to open employers' doors to Negroes. Finally, Minneapolis had a brand new Fair Employment Practices Commission, which was backed by an ordinance banning discrimination in employment. The neophyte Commission was just beginning to enforce that law by negotiation and exploration with employers. Other organizations may have existed, but these were the ones whose efforts came to the attention of store managers and whose pressures were beginning to be felt.

What pressures were the managers most aware of? Which organizations impinged on them most, and what other external sources forced them to think about changing their policies? Table 8-1 lists the outside influences converging on the managers in 1949.

Despite the larger number of organizations active in Minneapolis, Table 8-1 shows (fourth footnote) that fewer inexperienced employers were considering integration of their sales forces in Minneapolis than in St. Paul.

Table 8-1

Sources of Pressure for Sales Employment Breakthroughs

PRESSURE SOURCE	EXPERIENCED EMPLOYERS MPLS.	ST. PAUL	INEXPERIENCED EMPLOYERS MPLS.	ST. PAUL
The Urban Leagues	86%	100%*	23%	33%†
Minneapolis organizations				
F.E.P.C.	43	—	5‡	—
Joint Committee on Employment Opportunity	29	—	18	—
Self-Survey	0	—	9	—
The breakthrough process				
Breakthroughs in other stores	29	17	23	17
Qualified Negro applicants	14	33	0	6
Successful Negro performance below the ceiling in the same store	0	17	5	11
Unorganized pressures				
Public opinion	29	0	5	6
Size of Negro trade	29	0	0	0
Total §	259%	167%	88%	73%
Number of managers	7	6	22	18

*Influence boomeranged in one case but did raise issue.

†Includes "Haven't put enough pressure to get Association of Commerce to take a stand" as one response.

‡"The proposed state F.E.P.C. law raised the issue in our minds."

§Percentages may total more than 100% since individual managers may report pressure from more than one source. In Minneapolis 59% of the inexperienced managers and 39% in St. Paul reported they had never considered hiring Negro salesgirls for any reason.

For office workers, too, the same pattern holds. Presumably, the larger Negro population in St. Paul and the larger size of the St. Paul stores made Negro employment a livelier issue there than in Minneapolis. These facts show that passing a fair-employment law does not automatically bring integrated employment closer.

One might have expected the success of the four Minneapolis employers of Negro clerical workers to have influenced a larger number of colleagues. That other managers were not seems to be the result of the lack of publicity given the clerical breakthroughs. If these employers' experience had been more widely known, a larger number of Minneapolis stores might have considered employing Negro office workers. But in 1949 the possibility of doing so had not occurred to three-fifths of the officials interviewed except as this study itself raised the question in their minds.

The total number of pressures per respondent in Table 8-1 was higher for Minneapolis than for St. Paul. The extra pressure was concentrated on a limited group of stores, especially department stores. This larger battery of influences had not yet reached a wider *range* of stores.

The Urban League

We are now ready to examine the contribution of specific agencies to managerial decisions to hire Negroes above the job ceiling. First in importance were the two Urban Leagues. All six St. Paul employers of Negro salesgirls and all the Minneapolis employers except one credited Urban League pressure in their decisions to break with precedent. One St. Paul employer reported that he had at first been favorably impressed by the League but that more recently he had begun to rebel at its "domineering" approach. The remaining 11 employers were unequivocally positive in their attitude toward League officials and their work.

Among these pioneering employers, the Urban League was mentioned four times as often as any other source of pressure. Among inexperienced managers, the League was also first, though the proportion was much lower, since half of them had given no thought to the matter. Listed in second place was the experience of other employers, which was itself an indirect result of League work. In both cities, the Urban League was thus pre-eminent in bringing the issue of Negro employment to the attention of management and in persuading management to give it a try.

The number of employers that reported Urban League contact was less than the number of visits that the League's industrial secretaries had actually made. Of the respondents, 23 recalled such visits. But League records indicated that almost twice as many stores had been solicited for sales jobs. In St. Paul, the industrial secretary visited 19 of the 21 stores in my sample. These contacts resulted in the employment of Negro salesgirls by four stores under the acknowledged impetus of the League work. Of the 15 who had not yet employed Negro sales personnel, only six recalled League visits. Three store managers and six personnel managers in the remaining stores had no knowledge or memory of contact by the Urban League. In Minneapolis, visits to 20 stores in my sample were made jointly by the industrial secretary of the Urban League and the chairman of the Joint Committee for Employment Opportunity. Six of these stores subsequently hired Negro salesgirls, and one had already done so at the time of the executive's visit. Of the 13 nonemployers, eight managers recalled the visit, but five did not. Not only were they unaware of the agency's educational efforts, but they also stated unanimously that hiring Negroes in sales positions had never been considered at all.

The Urban Leagues' detailed records of store visits are undoubtedly trustworthy. How, then, can we account for the failure of so many officials to recall those contacts? One personnel manager had been on the job only six months, so the contact had presumably been with his predecessor.[1] But the bulk of the discrepancy apparently occurred because

---

[1]Mobility of personnel destroys the effect of previous League work and indicates the necessity of League orientation sessions with new store officials as they arrive on the scene by transfer or promotion.

the League secretaries and I interviewed officials of different rank. Wherever possible, I interviewed the personnel directors directly responsible for hiring and supervising employees. However, the Leagues followed a different practice:

> We interviewed top management (not the personnel men) because a change of basic policy was involved. In general we got either "go ahead" responses or flat refusals. There was very little middle ground (Minneapolis Urban League industrial secretary).

Industrial secretaries in both cities reported that, where top managers were favorably disposed, personnel directors were promptly called in to share the discussion of policy changes. However, if store managers refused to consider hiring Negroes for above-ceiling jobs, personnel directors seldom heard of the interviews and were thus impervious to the influence of the Urban League. It is therefore misleading to say that an Urban League official contacts a store as such. Rather, his contact is with individual officials, and relatively little influence filters down the hierarchy without transmutation in the process. Viewed from the lower ranks, pressure on top management appears as managerial liberalism, behind which the original Urban League initiative drops from sight.

According to *The Negro Worker in Minnesota* (1945), "the Urban Leagues in the two cities are organizations . . . [whose] almost exclusive concern is that of widening the job opportunities for Negroes." The two local chapters differed, however, in concentrating on new jobs to the exclusion of routine job-filling. The St. Paul organization had a definite policy governing the use of its limited resources:

> The St. Paul League specializes in skilled and semiskilled jobs. Placement of domestic workers has been turned entirely over to the United States Employment Service. Many St. Paul college graduates are working as red caps and in other railroad jobs. The Urban League is interested in upgrading them and in breaking down the job barriers.[2]

Since janitorial work is "Negro work," which Negroes can easily secure, no special assistance from the Urban League is necessary. The Government employment service can make such placements more easily. Because the St. Paul League staff was limited to two professionals and one stenographer, a policy of specializing in raising the job ceiling made it possible to apply leverage where it counted the most.

The St. Paul Urban League experimented with a group approach to employers. An informal meeting was arranged between Urban League staff members, a few League board members of high social status, and the owner-managers of four large department stores. League executives presented a carefully documented case for the employment of Negro salesgirls. Em-

[2]Interview with St. Paul Urban League executive secretary, July 28, 1949.

ployers were given ample opportunity to discuss the issue. After this meeting, one of the managers was the first in either city to break the ceiling, and the other three followed suit within a few months.

Robin Williams suggests the value of this group strategy:

> Changing the attitudes of groups rather than isolated individuals is the more effective approach for breaking up intergroup stereotypes and prejudices.
>
> . . . . Many stereotypes and dislikes are anchored not so much in the individual's personality as in the face-to-face groups to which the individual belongs and which determine his standards and ideals.[3]

Both the economics of competition and the equality of social and occupational status among department-store heads made this particular grouping of managers appropriate. Competitors are influenced more by each other's attitudes than by members of the lower ranks of their own organizations. Hence, decisions to embark on new hiring policies come more easily after group consultation than after employers are approached individually.

Whether in groups or separately, employers were subjected to various kinds of propaganda. The Minneapolis Urban League relied on idealistic appeals, whereas the St. Paul League used factual approaches. Minneapolis employers were confronted with such values as Americanism, patriotism, equality of opportunity, justice, and fair play. St. Paul employers, by contrast, were shown statistical charts and graphs of the poverty and disease in the Negro community.

The League published case histories in the St. Paul newspaper.

> Ann ————— is 24 years old, attractive appearance and appealing personality.
>
> Always interested in styles and salesmanship, she followed these subjects closely while finishing her high school course.
>
> Ann ————— is now a saleswoman for a large department store. . . . The fruit of years of research and conferences by the St. Paul Urban League, . . . the fruit of an employer's change of heart, his courage to upset the status quo, his willingness to put theory into actual practice.
>
> On her first day at work, who was more afraid, Ann or her boss? Both won't easily forget their nervousness.
>
> How has the experiment worked out? Employees get along well with Ann. Customers have commented favorably and Ann's sales are consistently high.
>
> Her dreams have come true. And her employer has the satisfaction of knowing that his shop does not deny anyone the right to earn a living.[4]

This write-up shows that the St. Paul office did not eschew all reference to ideals. Nevertheless, the two campaigns differed in emphasis.

---

[3]Williams (1947). In the second paragraph, Williams is quoting from Kurt Lewin (1946).

[4]"More Case Histories" (St. Paul Urban League, n.d.). (Mimeographed.)

Sociologists disagree about the effectiveness of various propaganda themes. Williams (1947) implicitly approves the case-history technique.

> Hostility is decreased by any activity which leads members of conflicting groups to identify their own ... life-activities in individuals of other groups. To be most effective this requires devices for inducing *personal* identification before the introduction of group labels.

Personalization is achieved to a high degree in Urban League stories of skilled Negroes who have been denied jobs that they were capable of handling.

Further support for a factual approach appears in Merton's discussion (1949) of the "propaganda of facts": "Propaganditis has reached epidemic proportions. Any statement of values is likely to be tagged as 'mere propaganda' and at once discounted."

In his communications research, Merton (1949) found "a central interest in *detailed circumstantial facts.*" When these are provided in propaganda,

> *the fact, not the propagandist, speaks. . . . The concrete incident, rich in circumstantial detail, serves as a prototype or model which helps orient people toward a part of the world in which they live. It has orientation value.*

In the same way, the St. Paul League's charts, graphs, and stories help orient busy executives with respect to an aspect of their local community about which they previously knew little or nothing.

"Technological propaganda" is apt to be effective even among propaganda-sensitive persons because it allows free choice.

> The propaganda of facts does not seek so much to tell people where to go, but rather shows them the path they should choose to get there. It preserves the individual's sense of autonomy. . . . The decision is voluntary, not coerced. . . . The cumulative force of facts carries its own momentum. . . . It is virtually a syllogism with an implicit conclusion —a conclusion to be drawn by the audience, not by the propagandist. . . . The voluntary drawing of conclusions has little likelihood of the aftermath of disillusionment which so often follows upon the propaganda of exhortation (Merton, 1949).

Technological propaganda also changes attitudes because "attempts to reduce intergroup hostility by education will be the more effective, the more the learners are convinced in the beginning that they themselves are not under attack for their opinions . . ." (Merton, 1949). The propaganda of facts provides a roundabout, nonaggressive approach.

Williams (1947) appears to disagree with Merton:

> In intergroup relations, as in many others, propaganda which makes an "emotional" appeal (value-oriented) is likely to be more effective than that which is restricted to factual appeal.

But later Williams (1947) qualifies this thesis:

> Appeals to conscience or ethics must be carefully handled, if they are
> to diminish rather than intensify hostility. In general, such appeals are
> probably most effective in reinforcing the sentiments of persons who
> are already convinced; they are probably not effective (immediately,
> at least) with militant anti-ethnics, and may even result in increased
> hostility as a reaction to guilt-feelings. That is, where individuals are
> utilizing prejudice to satisfy strong emotional urges, activation of the
> conscience-functions may tend to heighten psychological conflict and thus
> to result in increasingly devious or irrational hostilities.

A value-oriented approach is a dangerous tool if it is liable to boomerang.[5]

The Twin Cities managers characteristically cited values rather than facts
in analyzing their own motives for liberalizing their hiring practices. At
the conscious level, at least, ideological motives seemed salient. That the
managers frequently referred to values when interpreting their own behavior does not necessarily mean that value-oriented propaganda was more
effective with them. The managers pointed with pride to their own behavior as patriotic and democratic. But when the values theme appears in
race-relations propaganda, that theme implies that those to whom it is
directed are guilty of failure to live up to the American Creed. Values may
motivate these businessmen, but if values are thrown up to them by anyone
else, the result is apt to be defensiveness.

The Urban Leagues did not confine themselves to propagandizing. Within
the climate of opinion created by propaganda, the Leagues channeled
Negro applicants to likely firms. For the individual Negro in search of a
job, the League acted as a placement agency. For the manager willing to
employ a Negro salesgirl, the League screened candidates for the position and
thus saved personnel managers much of the burden of selection.

Steering Negro job-seekers to new stores might supplement verbal propaganda more effectively. During my interviews, a common escape route
for stores that had not employed Negroes was the fact that qualified
Negroes had never applied. Many managers had never had any Negro,
regardless of qualifications, ask for a job above the ceiling. Lacking applicants, managers could feel that Negro sales and clerical work was not an
issue.

Urban League officials had visited 35 Twin Cities managers without
skilled Negro employees. Half of those managers (17) told me that they
had never had any Negro apply for a skilled job. More strikingly, three
St. Paul and six Minneapolis employers stated explicitly that they were

---

[5]Although evidence on the effects of the two sorts of propaganda was not sought in
this research, the store managers had plenty of opportunity to report negative reactions to League propaganda. No criticisms were made. Lacking data, my discussion
is purely theoretical.

willing to hire Negroes for sales and/or clerical jobs but had never had qualified applicants.

When confronted with these facts, Urban League officials responded that 'they had offered to provide Negro candidates whenever a store indicated its willingness to hire Negroes. However, to require a categorical commitment is to expect too much of employers. A personalized approach would confront them with the visible challenge of skilled individuals applying for jobs. The verbal propaganda of facts communicated by Urban League visits could be reinforced by a "propaganda of persons," via qualified appli-. cants. Managers prefer to hire individuals without committing themselves to generalized policies and are unconvinced by talk when they have never met Negroes qualified for, or interested in, retail jobs. Only when verbal propaganda is reinforced by repeated applications from qualified Negroes are managers likely to see the issue as more than academic.

Though the Urban Leagues briefed Negro salesgirls on how to deal with customers, an aggressive policy of applying for retail jobs would require similar training in how to sell oneself to an employer. Drake and Cayton (1945) suggest that "Negroes have to acquire a technique in such matters. In particular, colored job applicants have the special problem of learning how to 'go back for more' when they have been rebuffed." Even managers known to be unsympathetic to Negroes can be impressed by direct contact with qualified individuals.

A third Urban League employment service was the supervision and disciplining of Negro employees of various companies. I have already cited an instance in which Urban League intervention might have prevented a new Negro salesgirl from misinterpreting the criticism of her fellow employees. Troubleshooting is a free insurance policy that the League provides to hesitant employers.

Depending on a particular manager's attitude toward the employment of Negroes, the Urban League can be seen as a pressure group or as an employment resource. Most breakthrough employers of Negro salesgirls utilized Urban League facilities for screening applicants. Pressure was reflected in such comments as "They kept insisting. They sent someone over, but we hired someone else" and "They kept trying to see if they could get someone in a sales position." Another manager, who reported that "they haven't put enough pressure on the Association of Commerce to get it to take a stand," implied that it would be reassuring to have official backing for action by his own store.

Only one manager was openly hostile to the Urban League:

The Urban League monopolizes Negroes; it takes the screening authority away from the store and is always suspicious of the store. Our company wanted to select our [Negro employees] for ourselves. We wanted only permanent resident. The Urban League couldn't be convinced why we didn't accept some of the transients they sent out. They suspected us of prejudice. We found the United States Employment Service a better source because we could specify what we wanted.

In contrast, a remarkable number of managers volunteered favorable comments on the services provided by the industrial secretaries.

During the postwar years covered by this study, the Urban Leagues made steady progress toward equal job opportunity for Negroes. With a full-time industrial secretary in each city, equipped with office space and secretarial help and assisted by full-time executive secretaries, and given long years of acquaintance with local conditions and the backing of a national organization, the Leagues were conspicuously important to the store managers. No other agency concentrated such extensive resources on the task of raising the Negro job ceiling.

The Joint Committee for Employment Opportunity

In May 1947, representatives of nearly 50 civic clubs and groups in Minneapolis formed the Joint Committee for Employment Opportunity. The purpose of the Committee was to mobilize consumer support for jobs for Negroes and other minority-group members in consumer service and retail enterprises. The Committee hoped to supplement the work of the local Fair Employment Practices Commission:

It is true that we have in Minneapolis an F.E.P.C. ordinance which makes it unlawful for a person to be denied employment because of his race, creed, or color. But we cannot blame merchants and employers entirely for discrimination in employment; no matter how idealistic they may be or how anxious to comply with the law, it is natural that they should not wish to jeopardize their business by attempting an innovation that they fear the public may not be ready to accept. If we therefore think in terms of enforcement alone, we might realize only a grudging compliance with the law.[6]

The Committee used two unique methods, a mass petition and envelope stickers. The Committee obtained the signatures of 10,000 people on a statement affirming their willingness to be served by any employee regardless of his race or religion and promising to patronize companies that hire minority persons in above-ceiling positions. This petition was presented to the Mayor's Council on Human Relations. The second device, a sticker encouraging equality in employment (to be affixed to statements when bills were paid by mail), was sold by the tens of thousands. In addition to these special projects, the Joint Committee for Employment Opportunity reinforced the Urban League by volunteering its own chairman to accompany the industrial secretary on visits to local employers.

[6]"History and Aims of the Joint Committee for Employment Opportunity," revised February 8, 1949. (Mimeographed, three pages.)

The Committee claimed considerable credit for the effectiveness of its program.

> *As a result of this program*, nine young Negro women are now successfully employed in six of the Loop stores as sales persons, a classification hitherto closed to them. (Emphasis added.)

In a later bulletin, however, the Committee gave supplementary credit to the follow-up work of the Urban League.[7]

Of the seven employers in my sample who had been persuaded to employ Negro salesgirls, only two mentioned the Joint Committee for Employment Opportunity. One manager recalled the visit of the J.C.E.O. chairman with the League official but made no mention of the petition or sticker campaign. Of 22 inexperienced respondents, four acknowledged the Joint Committee for Employment Opportunity by checking it on my list of influences. One personnel manager had heard of the organization and thought it had contacted the district manager. This personnel manager said that his superior had "asked me to give them cooperation." Another personnel manager had encountered the Committee at a meeting of the Board of Directors of the Retail Sales Association. He said that employing Negroes was not being considered for his own store but that the Committee had at least "raised the question" for the community as a whole. A third store official checked without elaboration the J.C.E.O. as one of many factors that together "have influenced Minneapolis attitudes toward greater tolerance than there used to be." Only one of the 29 Minneapolis store officials mentioned the petition's 10,000 signatures, and he claimed to be unimpressed.

The influence of the Joint Committee for Employment Opportunity on most officials was at best indirect. In the few cases in which the Committee was mentioned, managers remembered best their personal contact with the Committee chairman. Not a single respondent mentioned the 30,000 stickers, and only one was sufficiently aware of the lengthy petition to refer to it.

How adequate were the methods adopted by the Joint Committee? Politicians usually pay little attention to petitions from constituents since signing a petition requires little effort and since many people sign petitions without reading them or knowing what they are signing. Presumably, businessmen are as skeptical as politicians. Perhaps, too, the petition would have been more dramatic if it had been placed in the laps of potential employers instead of with the already convinced Mayor's Council on Human Relations.

Retail bureaucracy minimizes the effectiveness of a sticker campaign. The

[7]"Bulletin of the Joint Committee for Employment Opportunity," May 24, 1949. (Mimeographed, three pages.)

median number of clerical employees in our Minneapolis stores was 16.
Every store manager had at least one executive subordinate and at least
one stenographer. Hence, officials in charge of employment policy seldom
had direct contact with incoming payments for routine bills. An occasional office girl may have noticed the stickers, but there was no evidence
that she ever mentioned it to her superiors.

Time and money might have been better spent if the J.C.E.O. had en-
couraged consumers to write or go individually to store managers to present
their concern. If more personal contacts had been made, the managers
would have been more conscious of consumer pressure. Nevertheless, the
Joint Committee on Employment Opportunity was one more source of
pressure for the employment of Negroes.

The Minneapolis Community Self-Survey of Human Relations

Even less salient in the hierarchy of influences on Minneapolis employers
was the Self-Survey, which was sponsored by the Mayor's Council on
Human Relations. Only two employers checked this item. Of these, the one
who gave details was the only respondent in the Twin Cities who might
be described as fully aware of the dimensions of the race problem.
Acknowledging general familiarity with the "survey of the Mayor's Commission," this manager specified its chief findings as "increasing tolerance toward Negroes and a performance record for Negro workers equal
to the average of whites." With this exception, the findings and recommendations of the Industry and Labor Committee of the Self-Survey do not seem
to have been communicated to the local retail managers who could have
utilized them.

The chief influence of the Self-Survey was on the committee members
who carried it out. One recommendation of the Industry and Labor Committee was "that sound state Fair Employment Practices legislation, with
enforcement powers, be enacted and judiciously administered."[8] According
to the executive secretary of the Mayor's Council on Human Relations, this
recommendation was not a foregone conclusion. Several prominent indus-
trialists' opposition to legislation changed to advocacy as a result of what
they learned about discrimination from the Self-Survey.

The Minneapolis Fair Employment Practices Commission

The most controversial race-relations agency in the Twin Cities was the
F.E.P.C. The Appendix gives both the complete text of the Minneapolis

[8]"Report and Recommendations of the Industry and Labor Committee of the Minneapolis Community Self-Survey of Human Relations" (n.d.—apparently 1948). (Mimeographed, seven pages.)

ordinance as revised in 1948 and a comparison of the original 1947 law
with laws adopted by other cities and states. The original Minneapolis law
failed to provide a number of the powers that were available to stronger
Commissions elsewhere.

A proposed ordinance was first submitted to the Minneapolis City Council in December 1945. "An impressive number of community organizations
and individuals" spoke for the bill at public hearings.[9] Although no one
opposed the bill at the hearings, the Council failed to act. According to the
F.E.P.C., this failure was the work of "the more conservative business
interests in the community," who were operating behind the scenes. The
law was finally passed on January 31, 1947, after pressure had been brought
to bear on the City Council by labor unions and other organizations.

The slow process of adoption was followed by equally slow implementa-
tion. Mayor Hubert Humphrey took three months to appoint the first Commission. Throughout 1947, the Commission limped along without funds and
relied on the staff services that were occasionally provided by the Mayor's
Council on Human Relations. When the City Council finally made its first
appropriation in December 1947, it was so inadequate ($3,475) as to re-
strict the executive director to quarter-time employment. The next year,
the appropriation was increased enough to enable the executive secretary
and the office secretary to work half-time.

The first executive secretary of the Minneapolis F.E.P.C. had served on
the staff of the national F.E.P.C. during the war and had been executive
secretary of the Mayor's Council on Human Relations in Minneapolis. As
in the Commissions elsewhere, the Minneapolis emphasis was on conciliation and education rather than more forceful approaches. During the first
few years, no public hearings were held, and little publicity was given to
the work of the Commission.[10]

Of 56 cases included in a report entitled "Cases Handled from June 1,
1947–December 31, 1948," the F.E.P.C. won settlements in favor of the
petitioner in only 19 cases. Of the remaining cases, 16 were dismissed,
usually because the charge of discrimination was found to be unjustified,
and the other 21 were still pending. In an early report entitled "Analysis
of Operating Experience," the Commission describes a major handicap:

. . . In most cases, the person bringing a complaint of discrimination
to the Commission no longer wants to secure employment with the employer complained against. In the majority of cases, the complainant tells
the Commission that he would like to have the policy of the party charged

[9]"Steps in Securing Adoption of Minneapolis Fair Employment Practice Ordinance"
(Minneapolis F.E.P.C. Office). (Mimeographed, one page.)

[10]Between 1945 and 1960, the New York State Commission for Human Rights handled more than 3,000 "probable cause complaints" (in which discriminatory practices
were found) but held only 29 public hearings (Morgan and Hill, 1964).

corrected for the sake of future applicants, but that he does not want
the job himself because he believes that the employer is prejudiced.
... In such cases, the best the Commission can do is to get a commitment from the employer that he will not discriminate in the future and
then to put the case in an "action deferred" category to await positive
proof that the employer has corrected his discriminatory policy.

A classification of cases handled from June 1, 1947 to June 30, 1949
(prepared especially by the F.E.P.C. office for this study) shows the breakdown by party charged (Table 8-2). Retail stores were charged with discrimination only four times, and only one of these cases involved a Negro.
One reason that the F.E.P.C. encountered so few cases involving retail
stores may be the fact that Negroes have traditionally sought employment
elsewhere (and hence have sometimes been refused it) in service industries,
where the bulk of F.E.P.C. cases were concentrated.

Table 8-2

Cases Handled in the First Two Years of a Municipal Fair Employment Practices Commission

EMPLOYERS		NUMBER OF CASES
Manufacturers		12
Service industries		30
especially		
hotels	8	
beauty shops	6	
dry cleaners	4	
restaurants	4	
Construction contractors		4
Insurance and finance companies		10
(chiefly Jewish applicants for clerical positions)		
Retail trade		4
(mostly department stores)		
Wholesale trade		2
Government agencies		10
federal	3	
state	1	
local	6	
LABOR UNIONS		2
EMPLOYMENT AGENCIES		1
	Total	75

Source: Minneapolis F.E.P.C., June 21, 1947–June 30, 1949.

As do other agencies, Fair Employment Practice Commissions make extensive claims for their accomplishments. Executives like to take credit for all
subsequent changes in employment patterns.[11]

MacIver's appraisal (1948) of the wartime national F.E.P.C. is reserved:

... The pragmatic test is whether the institutional controls [that govern-
ment] sets up further or retard the major ends to which it proclaims
allegiance and on the appeal to which it won a mandate from the people.
By this test the F.E.P.C. was, *within the limits of its means*, a reason-
ably successful experiment. F.E.P.C. had a share in the combination

---

[11]Between 1941 and 1944, Negro employment more than tripled in 31 plants that
were involved in hearings of the wartime national F.E.P.C., but Norgren and Hill
(1964) conclude that "shortage of manpower rather than committee action seems to
have been primarily responsible for the rise in Negro employment."

of forces that extended the economic opportunities of groups subject to discrimination.... And it did not create, by and large, unfavorable repercussions such as might militate against further advance in this direction. (Emphasis mine.)

On the national scale, as well as in Minneapolis, results cannot be expected when staff resources are inadequate. Laws are seldom self-enforcing.

The statistical record for the wartime federal Commission was "favorable" settlement of 36% of the 4,000 cases filed with the Commission each year (Norgren and Hill, 1964). In these successful cases, "the discrimination complained of was eliminated without hearings by patient informal methods of persuasion and conciliation" (Maslow, 1946).

Maslow believes that the precise cause of the effectiveness of the national Commission lay in its enforcement powers:

> But of course such conciliation was effective only because of the threat of public hearings, complaints to procurement agencies, or the invocation of vague and unfamiliar wartime sanctions.

This emphasis on the crucial role of the teeth in antidiscrimination legislation was carried even further in editorial comment in *The Progressive*:

> Running through the state-by-state report [is a] profoundly significant trend: While employers have complied almost without waiting for warnings or complaints, it is clear that the presence of enforcement powers has proved a potent influence in achieving the excellent results on record....[12]

On a national scale, Norgren and Hill (1964) blame the ineffectiveness of successive presidential committees on their failure to invoke penalties when other methods failed. This failure was most notably true under Republican President Eisenhower:

> The Eisenhower committee's preference for voluntarism became so well known to contracting agencies, employers, and unions that little heed was paid to its activities throughout most of its career.

Norgren and Hill also compare the effectiveness of New York's enforceable F.E.P.C. law with the unenforceable ones of Indiana, Illinois, and Missouri and find that, over the 1950–1960 decade, nonwhites in fair-employment jobs increased by 75% in New York but by only 34% in the other three states. Norgren and Hill attribute the net difference to the enforcement powers and enforcement activities of the New York Commission. Specifically, New York has appropriated funds for full-time commissioners and for a large compliance and enforcement staff of specialists that are dispersed in regional offices throughout the state. The New York Commission has utilized individual complaints as a springboard for changing the entire employment pattern of the companies involved. Moreover, the Commission

[12]Editorial, "Design for Decency," *The Progressive*, April 1950, p. 4.

has regularly followed up these changes to be sure they have been maintained. These vigorous staff activities have enabled the law to secure unusual success.

A Philadelphia F.E.P.C. ordinance was passed just a year after the Minneapolis law. In Philadelphia, too, the F.E.P.C. was credited with major changes in local employment practices.

> Conditions prior to the passage of the F.E.P.C. ordinance seemed to defy solution on a voluntary basis. Philadelphia Quakers, through their own agencies and with many other groups, had made extraordinary efforts in a long campaign to win over the large department stores to the policy of hiring Negro clerks and sales people. They had used the methods of gentle persuasion and unobtrusive conversations with business executives. . . .
>
> Stern's and Gimbel's went ahead with the experiment of hiring several Negroes in sales and clerical jobs and were satisfied with the results. But the other stores held back.
>
> The F.E.P.C. measure was introduced . . . early in January 1948. It was passed by unanimous vote the following March. . . .
>
> The time of guinea pig experiments and pilot projects was at an end. The Fair Employment law applied to 46,000 Philadelphia employers, and everybody was now in the same boat. Wanamaker's hired its first Negro in the personnel office right after the law went through, and for the Christmas rush of 1949 had 20 colored sales clerks. These changes were initiated by Wanamaker's without any intervention by the Commission.
>
> All the big department stores have joined Stern's and Gimbel's and Wanamaker's in hiring Negro sales clerks, and the city has accepted the innovation with a feeling of relief. One of America's largest insurance companies which could not be won over to hiring Negroes for clerical work before the law went into effect now puts them on the payroll without comment (Fowler, 1950).

These authors attribute the success of F.E.P.C. laws at national, state, and local levels to the veiled threat of legal sanctions.

A document entitled "Testimony in Support of the Minnesota Fair-Employment Practice Bill" contains one generalized and one local plaudit for F.E.P.C. Under the heading of "Results achieved through the work of Fair-Employment Practice Commissions" is the following assertion:

> . . . There is ample evidence that the passage of the fair-employment laws has been of major importance in breaking down barriers to the employment of minority group workers. Employment opportunities in retail and wholesale trade, in manufacturing, and in office and clerical jobs have been significantly expanded for minority workers by voluntary changes in policy by a great number of important employers, entirely apart from any specific complaints of discrimination handled by the commissions.

This belief in the extensive repercussions of limited F.E.P.C. action is exemplified in the document's analysis of the Minneapolis experience:

...The satisfactory adjustment of a single case often has a far-reaching effect on employment opportunities.... The first case brought before the Minneapolis F.E.P.C. was against a major Minneapolis department store. The satisfactory adjustment of this complaint initiated a series of events which ultimately led to the opening up of employment opportunities which had formerly been closed to minority workers in all the major department stores in the city and at all levels of training and skill.

This claim for the impact of the Minneapolis F.E.P.C. law must be viewed with caution, however.

Table 8-2 lists only four retail-trade cases as appearing before the Minneapolis Commission. Only one of these involved a Negro, who claimed discrimination after being denied employment as a waiter in a retail store. Through the intervention of the Commission, he was eventually given a job. According to the executive director of the Commission, this successful adjustment was "important in paving the way for the employment of Negro salesgirls in that store."

I have already described the important role of the Urban League in the employment of Negro salesgirls in the Twin Cities. I have noted, too, that one difficulty facing the F.E.P.C. was that a complainant seldom stayed around long enough to take a job in the company against which he complained. One Urban League official expressed his "doubt whether F.E.P.C. has ever succeeded in actually placing people in jobs." Actually, four cases, or 7%, of the 75 cases handled by the Minneapolis F.E.P.C. between June 1, 1947, and December 31, 1948, achieved a favorable settlement. This number is certainly not large, but it does show that the Minneapolis Commission occasionally succeeded in directly placing a specific person in a specific job from which he had previously been barred.

On the whole, however, the F.E.P.C. executive did not see job placement as a major function of the Commission. He remarked, "The F.E.P.C. is not a job placement agency. The F.E.P.C. wants to do more in the way of opening up new job opportunities. There is no harm in some duplication with the Urban League here." In comparing the ability of the League and the Commission to communicate with employers, the F.E.P.C. executive saw handicaps and assets on both sides:

> At the moment, F.E.P.C. is a bugaboo. We hope to break down this hostility and increase our presently poor influence by direct contacts of an educational nature with employers. At first we will probably get a worse reception than would the Urban League.
> The Urban League is sometimes handicapped because employers view it as a pressure group, whereas the F.E.P.C. can go in and say, "This is a matter of public policy." But since the Urban League secretary is a Negro, it is good for employers to meet him—he makes a good impression on them.

In view of some wild claims in F.E.P.C. literature, the following remarks of a League executive do not seem overly critical:

The effect of F.E.P.C. is salutary but indirect. There is a tendency of some people to give too much credit to F.E.P.C. Actually the changes since 1947 are due to a complex of factors. For instance the gains at the telephone and street-car companies were made before F.E.P.C. was passed.[13]

In day-to-day race-relations activities, the personnel of the two agencies work harmoniously together. It is chiefly when writing annual reports and testifying before the legislature that partisans are carried away by enthusiasm for their own organizations.

Three of the seven Minneapolis employers of Negro salesgirls credited F.E.P.C. as a responsible factor. However, only one of the 22 inexperienced respondents reported that the ordinance was predisposing his store to liberalize its hiring policy. Indeed, seven other factors were mentioned more often than the F.E.P.C. in influencing the inexperienced respondents.[14]

Surprisingly, one St. Paul respondent listed F.E.P.C. as a factor in his thinking. He reported that the introduction of a proposed law into the 1949 state legislature together with the public hearings and newspaper discussion "raised the issue in our minds." This recognition shows the positive, educational effect that an F.E.P.C. bill *may* have even though a legislature fails to pass it.

In Minneapolis the city ordinance was similarly educational. The assistant personnel manager of a department store specifically denied that the law forced him to hire Negro salesgirls, but he did give the law credit for "starting us thinking along these lines." The only inexperienced employer that mentioned the F.E.P.C. felt the law predisposed customers to be more open-minded toward Negro salesgirls. Another personnel manager contended that the law was not influencing her company (at the time of my survey, hers was the largest lily-white store in the Twin Cities). Nevertheless, she confessed that, among the staff, "we have had some discussion about the law at the time it was first passed." Moreover, she disclosed that she "would never feel the company could use too many, but *we probably could use one or two.*"

One personnel manager had detected an increased number of Negroes applying for sales jobs since the passage of F.E.P.C. This observation would be in line with my hypothesis that a fair-employment ordinance would encourage Negroes to apply for higher-status jobs. However, one manager's opinion is not enough for a community-wide generalization. Moreover, this official recognized that the Urban League had probably sent those Negroes to his personnel office.

---

[13]This remark should not be interpreted as implying that the Urban League is opposed to the F.E.C.P., for the law creates an atmosphere within which the work of the Urban League is facilitated.

[14]This does not mean that only one employer was being influenced by F.E.P.C. It does indicate that most of the respondents either were not considering Negro salesgirls at all or preferred to list other influences as more important.

In debates on the wisdom of passing fair-employment legislation, controversy centers around the forcing of employers to do something to which they are opposed. This theme is conspicuous in the managers' own attitudes toward such laws (see Chapter 9). In spite of the fact that many managers were quick to verbalize their opposition to the compulsory element in F.E.C.P. laws, and despite the fact that the Minneapolis law had been revised in order to strengthen its enforcement provisions, none of the employers who had never hired a Negro above the ceiling said he felt threatened. And of the seven respondents who had taken on Negro salesgirls since the law was passed, only one referred to force. Even this manager did not resent the "coercion" which the law had exerted on him. He remarked:

> The law forced our hand; it forced us to do things to which we had no great objection but which were too much trouble to bother with. It's always easier to hire whites because you don't have the extra problems involved. Without the F.E.P.C. and the Urban League we probably never would have bothered to hire Negroes in the new positions. We might even take on some more now if we were pushed into it.

This personnel manager recognized compulsion but philosophically accepted it as a legitimate community concern about the operation of his private enterprise. Because his staff was so large, he felt obligated to begin token employment of Negroes at higher levels. However, the existence of an F.E.P.C. law would not force him to take on still more Negroes. Only persistent follow-up contacts from the staff of the F.E.P.C. and/or the Urban League would push him into taking on more Negroes in the future.

The law's effect was primarily educational. The greatest interest was aroused when the law was first considered and passed. By midsummer 1949, however, few managers listed F.E.P.C. as a direct influence on their thinking and behavior. The majority of officials, whether they had or had not enlarged their job opportunities, failed to indicate that they had been influenced by the law. Some, indeed, confessed complete ignorance of its provisions.

Only one Minneapolis manager reported direct contact with F.E.P.C. A Negro had applied to the company for a below-ceiling sewing job. Because he had not been hired, he had complained to the F.E.P.C. As a result, the F.E.P.C. executive investigated the situation. The manager said, "We were able to convince him that we had not had an opening at the time." As a result, the case was dismissed. In view of the fact that this manager was the only Minneapolis respondent who had dealt directly with the F.E.P.C., it is especially interesting that he opposed the ordinance when it was first introduced but now listed himself as a supporter. "F.E.P.C. is all right," he said, "as long as it is handled right. It seems to be O.K. in its administration so far."

Another Minneapolis employer commented on his shift from neutrality to support for the local ordinance by saying that in 1947 he was afraid of difficulty in its administration which would lead to increased resentment toward Negroes. However, he noted that "the law is being administered well."

Two other executives who commented on the record of F.E.P.C. had found nothing to change their original views. One consistent supporter said that the law is "working out fine here in Minneapolis." The other, who had always been neutral toward the law, revealed that, while "everyone in the company agrees to the basic principle, the fear is regarding the administration of the law"; the administration "could be a fiasco." His basic principle in evaluating the law was that, "if they're going to handle it right, it's O.K." According to his evaluation, F.E.P.C. "has worked moderately well."

In spite of widespread managerial opposition to F.E.P.C., only one respondent based that opposition on local experience. This official, who had been promoted to personnel work just six months before, contended that the local law had "forced the issue" and that the situation "left alone would have worked out better." This comment was not so much a criticism of the operation of the Minneapolis ordinance as a reflection of the widespread managerial conviction that such problems ought "to be handled individually" rather than subjected to governmental intervention and control.

Further favorable testimony on the operation of the ordinance was presented by Bradley L. Morrison, associate editor of *The Minneapolis Tribune*, in an article called "How F.E.P.C. Ordinance Is Working Successfully in Minneapolis," published March 16, 1949:

> . . . The work of the Commission . . . is not spectacular. It is not remaking the city overnight. Most employers probably do not give the F.E.P.C. a great deal of thought.
>
> But little by little, it is leaving an imprint on employment policies. The lines of discrimination are being pushed back slowly, and with a minimum of coercion and bad feeling.
>
> It is true that many employers do not approve of the F.E.P.C. They remain skeptical of any attempt, as they put it, to "legislate tolerance." But their original fears of the F.E.P.C. as an autocratic and trouble-making body have not been fulfilled.

George Jensen, an employer himself and the first chairman of the Commission, wrote in similar vein to a Minnesota state senator:

> A number of employers here in Minneapolis have expressed to me the conclusion that, although in some quarters of their organizations the idea of legislation of this nature has been resisted, compliance has proven that many of the ill effects expected from the legislation have failed to develop.[15]

[15]Letter dated February 9, 1949, "Testimony in Support of a Minnesota Fair Employment Practices Bill" (n.d.), p. 22. (Mimeographed.)

For employers who chose to comment on the operation of the Minneapolis ordinance, we can generalize that most reactions were favorable. Where shifts in attitude occurred, they universally involved increased support. Most employers, however, expressed no specific judgment of the Commission's work. Indeed, many admitted that they paid little attention to its work and knew little or nothing of it. Whereas ignorance of the provisions of the law was common, unawareness of the administrative record of the Commission was even more frequent.

Perhaps ignorance of the law's theory and practice is one reason for the statement of many personnel managers that the law had made "no difference in our thinking." Several respondents took pains to explain why the F.E.P.C. had *not* affected their thinking. Most asserted that their company policies had always been liberal, so no push was needed from government. One manager had voluntarily up-graded a Negro girl to a clerical position and was perhaps justified in saying that the law "has affected only those places which have discrimination." Another cited the company's all-Negro janitorial staff of 28 to prove that the law was not needed for his firm. While this company had only recently introduced Negro girls in customer-contact (fountain) positions, the sole acknowledged effect of F.E.P.C. was a change in application forms (presumably to remove questions about race, religion, or ethnic origin). A manager who had a large Negro janitorial and service staff but who had not yet hired any of the Negroes applying for sales and clerical jobs said that the law "hasn't made a change. ———————— Company has always been fair. In Chicago we have some all-Negro stores."

Another store official had no Negroes on his staff of 45 (although two were employed in "other service" capacities around the time of World War I). He contended that the law "doesn't make any difference" because "there is no discrimination in Minneapolis" and because "you can get around a law." A personnel manager who admitted complete ignorance of the details of the law claimed that her employment policies had not been affected "because we're not unionized in any way—unions tend to enforce such laws." She hastened to add that "we stay within the law regarding minimum wages, etc." But she nevertheless invoked her own rabid attitude toward unions when asked whether F.E.P.C. had influenced her thinking.

The "exempt" feeling of these six Minneapolis employers usually stemmed from a sense of harmony with the purposes of the law, but this feeling could arise when a manager was unaware of the provisions of the law or of the existence of discrimination in employment.

The Minneapolis Commission, at the time of the research, was aware of the need for intensifying its work. The Industry and Labor Committee of the Minneapolis Self-Survey recommended

that the Minneapolis Fair Employment Practice Ordinance . . . be given wide publicity as to its contents and purposes; further that employers, unions, and recruitment agencies be fully informed as to its progress to the end that the public as a whole will give its whole-hearted support to the ordinance and its effective administration.

Publicity was needed to reach the large number of Minneapolis personnel managers who were ignorant of the provisions of the law and even less aware of the accomplishments of the Commission.

Conferences with employers would have reduced the 45% and 59% of employers in the Minneapolis sample who had given no consideration to hiring Negroes in sales or clerical positions respectively. Pamphlets on techniques of integrating minorities would have reduced employers' fears of the untried. Informing minority groups about F.E.P.C. would have increased the number of Negroes who applied for skilled jobs and thereby reinforced the propaganda work of the executive director with employers. A vigorous and extensive program would have to have been carried on for several years before the new F.E.P.C. could have become effective in the community. Without such a program, it was still true in Minneapolis, as in the country as a whole, that "the right to a job has never been established as a civil right. . . . Employers have jealously guarded their right to hire and fire on any grounds they chose to cite" (Drake and Cayton, 1945).

Up to 1949, the Minneapolis experience with F.E.P.C. illustrated the following principles:

> First, that to expect discriminatory practices to be abandoned as a result of "educational" efforts alone is utopian.
> Second, that mere enactment of laws is not sufficient to put into motion the coercive powers of the state. . . .
> Third, that even well-conceived statutes are meaningless, unless groups most directly concerned with improving race relations exercise constant vigilance to . . . ensure adequate enforcement (Maslow, 1946).

The Domino Theory of Employment Breakthroughs

One store was persuaded to give Negro salesmanship a try and two others to integrate their offices as a result of creditable performances by Negroes in below-ceiling jobs. Four more stores were thinking of raising the ceiling for the same reason. On each occasion when stores acted on this motive, the manager up-graded a valued employee, typically a stock or elevator girl. Having assured himself of the girl's personality, ambition, and trustworthiness in an ordinary job, the manager was ready to risk placing her in an extraordinary job.

The successful experience of four Minneapolis stores with Negro office workers was not known to any other stores. Even within this group of pioneering managers, the three newcomers were unaware of the ten-year record of their forerunner.

At the time of this survey, not many above-ceiling jobs were open to

Negroes, but employers were beginning to hire Negroes as salesgirls. Consequently, several personnel and store managers had chanced to see Negro
salesgirls in other stores. And since the sales integration of Negroes resulted
from a pressure campaign, this new hiring trend received more publicity
by word of mouth and in print than the hiring of Negroes for other
types of jobs did. Three managers who had already employed Negro salesgirls and eight others who were considering doing so credited their knowledge of the favorable experience of other employers as a factor in their
own decision. Managers ranked this dynamic factor second, surpassed only
by the Urban League. Since the Urban Leagues were chiefly responsible for
the girls' employment in the first place, this ranking shows the secondary
gains that result from initial breakthroughs; nothing succeeds like success.

In Minneapolis two employers of Negro salesgirls revealed that their
new ventures were a joint undertaking of the major department stores.
Indeed, one of the managers added that "we've been trying to keep our
proportion down to that of the other stores." No doubt the experience of
those stores that broke the ice made it easier for others to follow.

Knowledge of the successful experience of the big department stores was
not limited to the 11 managers who were favorably impressed. The managers
of five other Minneapolis stores were fully aware of the Negro salesgirls
in local stores but considered them irrelevant because of differences in
type of store. The managers of a suburban department store, a furniture
store, and three women's clothing stores felt that their location and/or
selling relationships differed sufficiently from the big department stores to
create special problems if they employed Negro salesgirls. Another manager
said that, "if our competitors [the other variety stores] would do it, we
would follow the trend. But none of our competitors at present" is hiring
Negro salesgirls. The ice must be broken anew, it appears, for each new
type of store.

Negro pioneering in new situations sometimes has widespread repercussions. Many managers mentioned Jackie Robinson, who had just become
the first Negro member of a major-league baseball team. Their imagina-
tion had been captured by the widely publicized story of his skill, hard
playing, and even temper under provocation. Many managers considered
Robinson an example of a Negro making the best of a new situation, an
indication of the likelihood of favorable customer acceptance, and a sign of
the trend of the times. The pioneering of baseball manager Branch Rickey
in New York made it easier for Twin Cities store managers to pioneer.

The Role of Pressure

Two respondents spoke of a general shift in "public opinion" as a factor
in their decision to hire Negro salesgirls. Only one manager in the whole
sample reported individual pressure that was unchanneled through any

organization; inquiries had come from both white and colored customers
and from Negro elevator operators about the possibility of Negro girls
in sales positions. Two other employers felt they had enough Negro customers to justify having Negro salesgirls.

With these few exceptions, the outside pressure felt by Twin Cities employers came entirely from organized sources, chiefly the Urban Leagues,
but supplemented in Minneapolis by the F.E.P.C. and the Joint Committee
for Employment Opportunity. This pressure was not coercive. No managers
felt threatened by either the implied possibility of economic boycott in the
consumer approach of the J.C.E.O. or the minor fines and imprisonments
which the F.E.P.C. was authorized (but was unlikely) to impose. Rather,
pressure took the form of consultation and negotiation between representatives of agencies concerned with minority groups and officials of retail
business. This persistent effort to explore the possibility of new jobs for
Negroes, to offer advice and assistance in the selection and placement
of such workers, and, in the case of the F.E.P.C., to investigate specific
charges of discrimination, brought the results I have recorded.

No one agency deserves all the credit for these achievements. While there
were occasional tensions between the pressure organizations, the general
pattern was cooperation in a concerted drive to secure sales jobs for Negroes. Even where cooperation was not explicit, each agency reinforced
the others. Thus pressures piled up. Even though the average employer
preferred to credit himself with liberalizing his employment policies, many
managers admitted that the Urban League, the F.E.P.C., and the Joint
Committee on Employment Opportunity provided the impetus for their decisions.

Pressure was unspectacular but nonetheless essential to raising the job
ceiling. The Negro community was too tiny a minority to hope that its needs
would be felt by the dominant group except through diligent efforts at
communication via personal conferences and published literature.

> The average Northerner does not understand the reality and the effects
> of such discriminations as those in which he himself is taking part in
> his routine of life. To get publicity is of the highest strategic importance
> to the Negro people (Myrdal, 1944).

In view of the Twin Cities employers' reluctance to take even minimal
risks, outside pressure was an essential factor in improving job opportunities
for Negroes. Indeed, it seems unlikely that, apart from the initiative of
these outside agencies, any Negro salesgirls would have been hired in
Minneapolis or in St. Paul.

Many years ago, in 1929, the industrial secretaries of 15 Urban Leagues
drew up a list of means by which Negroes had broken through job ceilings
in industry. Among them were "the practice of passing for white; political
influence; . . . accepting completely segregated facilities; accepting lower

pay; opportunism; ... strike breaking" (Johnson, 1930). I quote these six items from the total list of 12 because they differ so sharply from the means employed in the Twin Cities. The pressure campaign that opened up jobs in more than a dozen stores where they never existed before required no sacrifice of Negro self-respect or of labor standards. Outside pressure and internal conditions persuaded the managers to open up new job opportunities. But, so far as could be ascertained, the pressures left few residues of resentment and dissatisfaction. These changes in the pattern of Negro employment in the retail stores opened the door to further assaults on the job ceiling. They rested on a foundation of support in law (in Minneapolis) and organized interest groups, in customer and employee acceptance, and in employer satisfaction. In short, organized pressure groups had scored a solid victory.

Chapter 9

F.E.P.C. as a Political Issue

The previous chapter's record of Minneapolis employers' practical experience with the F.E.P.C. law provides a background for studying the same men's political attitudes toward the F.E.P.C. idea. I expected the Minneapolis employers who originally opposed the F.E.P.C. ordinance to change their minds as a result of first-hand experience, to come to approve the law, and to advocate its extension to the state level. St. Paul employers, who lacked experience with the law (and especially those without experience in employing Negroes) were expected to oppose F.E.P.C. legislation at both the local and the state level.

Minneapolis employers were asked their attitude toward the local ordinance not only as of the time of the interview but also before the law was passed in 1947. This dual approach was designed to locate attitude changes that resulted from experience with the ordinance in operation.

Table 9-1

Managers' Attitudes toward Local, State, and National F.E.P.C. Laws, by City

	ATTITUDE TOWARD LOCAL, STATE, OR NATIONAL F.E.P.C. LAW, BY CITY					
	LOCAL F.E.P.C.		STATE F.E.P.C.		NATIONAL F.E.P.C	
ATTITUDE	MPLS.	ST.P.	MPLS.	ST.P.	MPLS.	ST.P.
Strongly, publicly support	0%	14%	0%	14%	0%	14%
Support	43	14	43	24	17	10
Neutral	17	24	10	19	10	19
Oppose	34	38	43	33	47	47
Strongly, publicly oppose	0	0	0	0	3	0
Don't know	3	5	0	5	20	5
Not ascertained	3	5	4	5	3	5
Total	100%	100%	100%	100%	100%	100%
Number of managers	30	21	30	21	30	21

Critical ratio = 1.09, P > .20 for differential support of local versus national F.E.P.C. ordinance.

We have already seen that few managers had any direct contact with F.E.P.C. in operation. In view of the general lack of knowledge about the operation of the law, it is not surprising that only two managers changed their views. Both increased their support for the law; one shifted from opposition to support, the other from neutrality to support.

While a Minneapolis plurality supported the local ordinance, a St. Paul plurality opposed a local law. The significance of this difference between the two cities is diminished by the fact that half the St. Paul supporters were "strong and public" advocates of fair-employment legislation for not only their city but also the state and the nation. No Minneapolis supporter took a public stand, while the only public opponent in either city opposed a national law alone and favored F.E.P.C. for his own city and state. One public supporter telephoned the Retail Trade Association to inform them that he "didn't want to have any part in [their] opposition to F.E.P.C." Another manager confessed that he did not know too much about F.E.P.C. but believed that he "*ought* to come out publicly for such legislation." Both confessed that much of their reason for a strong stand in favor of F.E.P.C. came from their minority identity as Jews. A third official who checked this strong response had not yet expressed herself publicly but wished to be recorded as strongly in favor of fair-employment legislation at every level.

Idiosyncratic rather than situational factors seem to have led these St. Paul managers to favor F.E.P.C. so strongly. Thus, their intensity does not seem to throw doubt on our generalization that Minneapolis employers were somewhat more favorable to F.E.P.C. because of their experience with it than their St. Paul counterparts, who had only viewed it from afar.

Attitudes toward potential state and national legislation were less consistent. The number of Minneapolis managers who opposed F.E.P.C. steadily increased from the local to the national level. The big shift came at the national level, when the supporting group made a net shift of six to "don't know" and of two to opposition. Opposition to federal legislation was almost as marked in St. Paul, but a slight, unexpected shift yielded net support of F.E.P.C. at the state level.

For the Twin Cities as a whole, F.E.P.C. was just barely favored at local and state levels, while national legislation was opposed by more than 2 to 1. For both state and federal laws, the managers were less sympathetic in Minneapolis than in St. Paul. This fact refutes my predicted carry-over of attitudes toward F.E.P.C. from the local level to broader jurisdictions. Although the state and national views of both the St. Paul and the Minneapolis managers reverse the local pattern, the percentage difference is smaller. Moreover, the individual companies are less directly involved in these more remote jurisdictions. Later analysis will show that the marked opposition of the Minneapolis employers to national legislation is the result of a pronounced sensitivity to the special racial situation facing the South rather than derived from local experience. It is noteworthy, however, that the preponderant sentiment in favor of the Minneapolis ordinance failed to affect attitudes toward legislation for wider jurisdictions.

A National Opinion Research Center poll of a nationwide sample of businessmen in 1945 showed that 57% opposed F.E.P.C.[1] Compared with this poll, my Twin Cities respondents were slightly more liberal; only 49% explicitly opposed national legislation.

Eleven months after my interviews were completed, the Minnesota Poll of Public Opinion announced the results of a state-wide sample of opinions on F.E.P.C.[2] To the question "Would you be in favor of such a law in Minnesota, or would you be against it?" the cross section answered "in favor," 75%; "against," 16%; "qualified," 3%; and "no opinion," 6%. This preponderant vote in favor of F.E.P.C. marked "a sharp reversal of sentiment within the last year and a half." In January 1949 the poll found that "55% of the adults interviewed . . . thought the state should take no action 'concerning employers who turn down job applicants on account of their race, religion, color or nationality.'" Only 30% at that time thought the state should act.

It is impossible to say whether a similar shift took place in the attitudes of retail managers, too. However, the 1950 poll showed (a) men, (b) Republicans, and (c) people over 50 years of age least favorable to a state F.E.P.C. Since most store managers fall in these categories, managers can be expected to be more conservative than the general public.

An official of the Minneapolis Urban League exaggerated managerial conservatism; he guessed that "nine out of ten" Minneapolis employers opposed F.E.P.C. He suggested that employers conform to group pressure: "Employers are supposed to be anti-F.E.P.C." From the Urban League perspective,

> employers blast the F.E.P.C. because they are afraid of it and don't want to get caught by it. They would rather work with the Urban League. Since "F.E.P.C." has become such a red-flag term, we're substituting the term "anti-discrimination legislation."

I originally hypothesized that there would be less opposition to F.E.P.C. among employers who had had Negro employees than among those without fair-employment experience. I assumed that favorable experience with Negro employees would liberalize a manager's attitude toward fair-employment legislation.

Cause and effect, however, are difficult to determine. If a manager feels strongly enough about fair employment to favor government intervention, he is likely to practice fair employment voluntarily. This generalization apparently describes the three Minneapolis employers who had voluntarily

[1]Schermerhorn (1949). A Harris poll 18 years later disclosed 62% support by whites nationally and 40% support by southern whites for a federal F.E.P.C. law (Brink and Harris, 1963).

[2]"State F.E.P.C. Law Favored by 75 Pct.," *Minneapolis Sunday Tribune*, July 30, 1950.

taken on Negro stenographers. The two managers with full-time Negro office workers consistently supported both local and state laws. For the national level, they were among those who shifted to "don't know." The third was a personnel manager who had given one girl some semiclerical record-keeping. This manager, too, supported state legislation and was not sure about federal legislation. However, she was neutral toward the Minneapolis law but said that she would support it with modifications.

In St. Paul, however (where I have interpreted the smaller support for a local ordinance as partly due to lack of experience with one), this relationship did not hold. The only employer who had had a Negro girl as combined switchboard operator and office worker opposed F.E.P.C. at every level on grounds of "impracticability" but admitted that "I may be wrong."

The attitudes of managers who hired Negro salesgirls, however, are more in accord with my hypothesis. The combined employment pressure of the Urban League, Joint Committee for Employment Opportunity, and F.E.P.C. pushed managers into changing their policies. Employers who hired Negro salesgirls under pressure illustrate the hypothesis that experience with Negro employees liberalizes attitudes toward F.E.P.C. laws. Of the Minneapolis managers who had employed Negro salesgirls, six were for, one neutral, and one against the local F.E.P.C. At the opposite extreme were four employers who had never employed Negroes at any job level; one was in favor, two were neutral, one was opposed, and one was uncertain. In St. Paul, the difference is less striking. Among St. Paul employers of Negro salesgirls, one manager favored, two were neutral, and one opposed F.E.P.C., while the single manager who had never hired any Negroes was consis-tently against F.E.P.C.

Further examination shows that these data are not conclusive. It is not the Minneapolis employers of Negro salesgirls who changed their attitudes toward F.E.P.C., but one of the voluntary employers of Negro office workers and that other manager who was vindicated by F.E.P.C. when he was charged with discrimination. Not one of the eight Minneapolis managers who had employed Negroes in sales positions during the previous two years changed his views as a result of that employment.[3] Moreover, no respondent in either city cited employment experience with Negroes as a basis for the desirability or practicality of fair-employment legislation. The few managers who did base their political ideas on practical experience referred to the way F.E.P.C. was administered in Minneapolis or elsewhere, rather than to the successful integration of Negroes into local sales forces.

Although there is a positive correlation between employing Negro salesgirls and supporting F.E.P.C., there is no evidence that the former pro-

[3]In St. Paul, I did not raise the question of changing attitudes toward F.E.P.C. that might have resulted from personal experience in employing Negroes.

duced the latter. We therefore cannot say that the correlation substan-
tiates the hypothesis that experience with Negro employees produces
support for fair-employment legislation or, conversely, that lack of experience
is conducive to opposition. We must conclude, contrary to my expectation,
that there is no observable carry-over from employment experience to managerial attitudes toward employment legislation. There does seem to be
room for the opposite kind of sequence; attitudes toward F.E.P.C., independently arrived at, may predispose employers to accept or reject Negro
applicants when those employers are not subjected to pressure and are
thus free to choose.

Company Policy toward F.E.P.C.

No respondent felt that the attitude of other officials, or "company
policy" on F.E.P.C., was more liberal than he himself was. Three thought
their colleagues less liberal, but 11 felt their associates shared their own
views. Political solidarity was particularly common among Minneapolis
supporters of F.E.P.C.; seven said company policy backed their own approval of the ordinance. An equal number of St. Paul respondents had no
idea how their fellows stood on the matter—perhaps because F.E.P.C.
was not yet a live issue in that city.

Although Minneapolis had an F.E.P.C. law, ignorance about company
policy was almost as widespread there as in St. Paul. Many respondents
had no positive knowledge but assumed their fellow managers would view
an ordinance the same way. In both cities the guesses and "don't knows"
indicate that F.E.P.C. was not a salient issue for most employers.

One manager who was himself "neutral" on F.E.P.C. said that company
policy was "pretty largely" the same as his own. But he added, "The
higher up you go, the more removed the official is from actual contact with
Negro employees, so the more opposed he is to F.E.P.C. and thinks in
terms of a 'big black buck nigger.'" This manager thought that his own
contact with Negro employees had replaced his stereotyped views of Negroes
as a race with personalized attitudes toward them.

Personal Positions on F.E.P.C.

In each city, one manager refused to comment on F.E.P.C. One said,
"I never express myself on political issues." When pressed by renewed
assurances of anonymity, he reiterated, "I never answer questions about
political issues." The other personnel manager indicated that he would
"rather not say" how he felt about the F.E.P.C. idea because "we stay
out of politics" and said that staying out was "official company policy."

The other 51 store officials were willing to commit themselves. Two
admitted that they knew so little about F.E.P.C. that "don't know" would

be the only honest response. Five listed their preferences but added such comments as "not too well informed on the law," "I haven't paid much attention to it," and "I know the law's in existence, but I feel removed from the problem." One personnel manager concluded the interview by remarking that "I guess I'll have to go and find out more about F.E.P.C. since I'm having such a hard time answering your questions."

Ignorance is often considered a source of opposition to laws like F.E.P.C. Our poorly informed managers were too few for safe generalization, but only one of them opposed a local F.E.P.C., one was neutral, and the other three were all sympathetic (one was even a "strong and public" supporter).

The Proponents

The American Creed

Support for fair-employment legislation was often expressed in terms of the American Creed. This idealistic argument was used by 12 respondents, whereas no other argument was mentioned by more than four. From the perspective of the effect of F.E.P.C. on minorities, the F.E.P.C. idea was described by one manager as an expression of democracy (but another manager labeled F.E.P.C. "undemocratic" because it curbs the freedom of businessmen). "It's fair," said three; "It's justice," said another. "They should have a fair chance," said two managers, while another said similarly, "They need a break." One manager believed in "equal rights," and another quoted the Declaration of Independence ("All men are created equal"). He called this idea "the American idea." One appealed to "equality of opportunity" and added that "individuals should be treated on their own merits." Four argued that "there shouldn't be any discrimination" and believed that F.E.P.C. was an essential means to achieving this end. In general, these managers based their arguments on the generalization that discrimination in employment violates the American ideal of equality of opportunity for the individual. Fair-employment-practice laws extend that ideal to members of minority groups. Therefore, F.E.P.C. should be supported.

Practical Values

Only a few practical arguments were marshalled by supporters. Two pointed out that F.E.P.C. was working well in Minneapolis, and one pointed to Boston. Two cited the educational effect of F.E.P.C.-motivated hirings on customers. A Minneapolis respondent commented, "The law enables customers to see that Negroes can do the job; it overcomes their ignorance." A St. Paul manager spoke conditionally: "F.E.P.C. would change customer reactions—with the law behind the store, they would accept Negro salesgirls." (This respondent, incidentally, did not know that Minneapolis already had an F.E.P.C. law.)

Twin Cities employers were divided in their evaluation of F.E.P.C. performance elsewhere. One manager said that "Boston has a good F.E.P.C. law" but claimed that employers there were getting around at least some of its provisions. Another said he had heard that every Boston store was compelled to hire a fixed percentage of Negroes, whether they were competent or not. Still a third contended that the New York law "hasn't resulted in any radical changes."[4]

In contrast to these varied appeals to experience is the attitude of the personnel manager of the pioneering Connecticut firm of Pitney-Bowes: "Many of the problems which we encountered would have been much less difficult had we had the support of legislation."[5] The same man made elsewhere a broader appeal for support of F.E.P.C.: "I think these laws are a very important step in the right direction. If they did nothing else, they would at least be helpful to those employers who would prefer to treat the Negro fairly, but who would lack the courage to do so without the excuse which the laws furnished."[6]

From Philadelphia comes a summary of interviews by Frank Loescher with executives of more than 100 firms:

> Only one employer refused to see him. The others were sympathetic and expressed the belief that there were Negroes qualified to handle a variety of jobs in his firm. But they were afraid their employees would object and that the business would lose money; they could not afford to act as guinea pigs in any such risky venture. Frequently a man would say: *"I would welcome a fair employment law because then I would know everyone would be doing the same thing"* (Fowler, 1950, emphasis added).

The beneficial impact of F.E.P.C. assumed by most Philadelphia employers and by two St. Paul employers (but by none in Minneapolis) must be qualified if it is to be more than wishful thinking. That qualification is the provision of a staff adequate to secure compliance with the law. Only then will the sequence foreseen by Myrdal (1944) come to pass:

> By attacking the color bars everywhere, it is possible to minimize the change needed in any individual establishment if the Negro is to be completely integrated into the economic system. The breakdown of discrimination in one part of the labor market facilitates a similar change in all other parts of it.

This potentiality is an important argument in favor of F.E.P.C., but only adequately equipped commissions can prove the validity of that argument.

[4]The previous chapter cited data from Norgren and Hill (1964) that suggested that in *subsequent* years the New York law produced "radical changes." However, 1949 was early in the experience of any of the Fair Employment Practice Commissions.

[5]"Does State F.E.P.C. Hamper You?", *Business Week*, February 25, 1950, p. 116.

[6]Minnesota Council for F.E.P.C., "Additional Testimony." Letter from J. J. Morrow, personnel manager of Pitney-Bowes, Inc.

The "practical" arguments for F.E.P.C. concerned the support and protection a law would provide an individual store during the transition to employment policies that benefit Negroes. No one argued that F.E.P.C. would be good for his store in anything other than a protective sense. Theoretically, someone could have argued that F.E.P.C. would widen the supply of skilled labor. But few Negroes were seen as being that useful. F.E.P.C. was good for democracy and good for the Negro—not good for business.

The Jewish Creed

Two managers argued from their own group involvement. "I'm in a minority myself. Therefore I have to believe in this." This remark gave the principal reason for a "strong and public" supporter's approval of F.E.P.C. Another Jewish employer found himself torn by conflicting views. He cited his minority status as responsible for his belief in "the principle" of F.E.P.C. but confessed his fear that such laws are unworkable in practice.

The Bandwagon

Six employers with varying personal attitudes toward F.E.P.C. felt that the trend locally and nationally was toward governmental action. "The law will probably come eventually," said one opponent of the legislative approach to fair-employment practices, while a supporter expressed the belief that "public opinion is pushing in that direction." One manager was philosophical about the whole affair: "It's a general social movement —can't really be resisted. Let's not make fools of ourselves." Another predicted a bandwagon effect: "As the movement grows, recalcitrants will swing over."

The Opponents

Opposition to F.E.P.C. was phrased in three themes: free enterprise, boomerang effects, and unenforceability.

Free Enterprise

It is understandable that, in the McCarthy era of self-conscious reaction against communism, slogans of free enterprise should come easily from the managers. Like the manager who called F.E.P.C. "undemocratic," a sizable group saw legislation as an unjustified interference in the proper province of the businessman. Many managers assumed that hiring Negroes above the job ceiling would jeopardize the smooth functioning of an enterprise; hence, government ought to refrain from such uneconomic (or at least non-economic) meddling. These ideas ranged from vague generalities to specific predictions.

One young official, who had been in personnel work only a month, developed this theme at length.

No group should tell business how to operate. If the businessman is trying to make a profit, he shouldn't have any interference. We are getting too much government control of everything in the United States. This country was built on private enterprise.

Another contended that, "if business is to survive, it must be allowed some freedom for initiative." F.E.P.C., to these men, was one more manifestation of "big government."

Others did not see so drastic a threat, but they resented losing control over an essential managerial function: "We wouldn't be free to use our own judgment. That wouldn't be quite fair. We would be governed. The Government shouldn't tell us what to do—we're entitled to our own opinions."

One manager described F.E.P.C. as "meddling in business, telling business whom they have to hire. Private business should be able to hire whomever they wish." Two mentioned "subtle factors" in individual personality that determine who is hired and added that it would be "embarrassing" to have to describe in a public hearing their reasons for not hiring an applicant who would not fit the job. Another saw F.E.P.C. as "a club over the employer's head, forcing him to hire someone he doesn't want." For example, "if a Negro girl with sales experience applied for a cosmetics sales position, she couldn't demonstrate to white customers how the cosmetics would look by putting them on her own face." Yet F.E.P.C. would stir up a lot of trouble if the company turned her down.

Closely related to this emphasis on managerial rights is the rejection of F.E.P.C. by five managers because it would be a nuisance. It would be "too much trouble to explain one's reasons for not hiring a particular person." It would be "too easy to bring groundless charges against the employer." Other managers feared publicity, which customers would interpret unfavorably even though the charges proved false.

Unenforceability

Of eight employers who contended that F.E.P.C. is unenforceable, seven claimed that employers can get around the law. The eighth divulged that "almost all Boston stores have private codes" for noting the race of applicants; these codes take the place of the outlawed questions on record forms. He pointed out that "small employers (under 50 employees) never advertise, so no one ever knows when the store has vacancies, and therefore discrimination can't be proved." Two employers resented the threatened interference of a law that, they also said, could be easily avoided. Their inconsistency implies that unenforceability may be simply a rationalization of opposition.

Four respondents based their prediction of unenforceability on the ground that race relations is an improper field for legislation. Two invoked the fate of the prohibition amendment. "You can't legislate friendship or emotions," said one. Another stated similarly, "I can't see the legislation of attitudes." Three managers agreed that you "can't legislate people into doing what they don't want to do."

Ranking first among arguments against F.E.P.C. was interference by big government in the domain of free enterprise and the fear that intervention would be a nuisance, disrupting smooth business operations. According to the opposition, the crucial danger lay in this threat to management prerogatives and to the network of employee and customer relations. Arguments that F.E.P.C. would be unenforceable or would have a negative effect on Negro welfare were light artillery brought up to reinforce managerial fears.

Managerial support of F.E.P.C. was based on benefit to minority groups. Opposition originated in anxiety about damage to one's own business. That anxiety must have been very convincing. The supporter threw his weight behind F.E.P.C. because he was a good citizen. The opponent took his stand because he wanted to be a good store manager. Only where a supporter acted from his status as a Jew was there a group involvement that approached the status-determined motivation of the opposition.

Many respondents were torn by the conflicting roles of being a citizen (and minority member) on the one hand and a manager on the other. Where the citizen role won out, the managerial role was seldom called into play. But where the managerial role determined overall opposition to F.E.P.C., the respondents found it necessary to appease the citizen status by contending that F.E.P.C. does not really work and would, after all, be bad for Negroes.

The Twin Cities opponents were joined by the editors of the reputedly liberal Louisville newspaper *The Courier-Journal.*

...A peace-time F.E.P.C. is an effort to legislate morals and social doctrine and is unenforceable, impracticable, conducive of tyranny on the one hand and evasion on the other. Moreover, we think it will harm the people it is intended to help. It is a field in which neither legislation nor fiat will substitute for the slower processes of education and attempts by the fair-minded men and women of both races to understand and sympathize with each other's points of view.[7]

The argument that F.E.P.C. is an affront to free enterprise is not subject to empirical test. The question involves a choice between values stemming from the American Creed and those of classical economics. Proponents say that an agency will not be likely to invade an employer's personnel office very often, but opponents resent *any* governmental intrusion. Up to August 1949, Minneapolis employers had had few grounds for complaint about interference. Similarly, on the more comprehensive scale of ten

[7]Editorial, "Let the F.E.P.C. R.I.P. This Session," *The Courier-Journal*, September 2, 1949.

states with fair-employment-practice laws, a survey conducted by *Business Week* concluded:

> Employers agree that F.E.P.C. laws haven't caused near the fuss that opponents predicted. Disgruntled job-seekers haven't swamped commissions with complaints. Personal friction hasn't been at all serious. Some employers still think there's no need for a law. But even those who opposed an F.E.P.C. are not actively hostile now (February 25, 1950).

More recently, Norgren and Hill (1964) point out that merely passing laws is not enough. Enforceability is possible but not automatic.

> The F.E.P.C. laws in effect in most Northern and Western states and in several major Northern cities have up to now resulted in only a very modest and spotty decrease in discriminatory employment practices. Nevertheless, the analysis of experience under these laws demonstrates that enforceable F.E.P.C. legislation, if properly designed and wisely administered, can be an effective means of combating racial discrimination in employment.

Greenberg (1959) similarly concludes that Fair Employment Practice Commissions change employment patterns "in proportion to their budgets and assiduity" and notes a marked increase in the effectiveness of the New York State Commission Against Discrimination under a more vigorous administrator.

Some of those who doubt the enforceability of F.E.P.C. deduce their skepticism from the thesis that attitudes cannot be molded by laws. This question is discussed by MacIver (1948):

> There are ... sociologists who claim that law cannot move ahead of the mores, that it can be effective only when public opinion is already so manifestly on its side that legal procedures merely give institutional form to custom.... [But] there are certain types of situations, where public opinion is divided, distracted, uncertain, or ambivalent, in which the passing of a law can be decisive. To this order belongs the situation ... of indifferent equilibrium.

We earlier applied the concept of indifferent equilibrium to employee attitudes on the integration of Negro workers. In that context, it seemed that strong management leadership should minimize difficulties. Twin Cities managers were similarly divided on the question of the unrestricted employment of Negroes; the managers were divided not simply into two camps but divided within themselves between their sense of oughtness about fair employment and their forebodings about what might happen to their stores if the ceiling were removed.

Noland and Bakke (1949) suggest that there is an overwhelming tendency for role conflict to be resolved in favor of the managerial role.

> ... This conception of the necessities imposed on them as leaders of the productive team handicaps management in certain respects in performing another role, *leaders in the community*.... Perhaps one cannot expect

that a majority of employers will put their community leadership role ahead of their enterprise leadership role and take the risk of social conflict in the work society for which they are primarily responsible. ... After all, the task for which management is primarily and most immediately rewarded or punished is promoting the welfare, not of the community, but of their own firm.

In view of the fact that the Twin Cities managers were more evenly divided over the propriety of fair-employment legislation than might be expected from the above statement, I raised the following questions of senior author Noland: Can the usually weak community demand for integration of minorities be strengthened to counteract the strong executive desire to minimize risk? Is it accurate to say that a firmly administered F.E.P.C. law constitutes one means of bolstering the community demand?

In reply, Noland agreed that a law can help throw the balance of opinion in the desired direction. He answered:

My study indicated *company welfare* ranked above *community welfare* in the employer's hierarchy of values. But the two are so closely related, that having things "all right" in the community situation would help make things "all right" at the plant. Therefore it would seem that (a) community insistence on the integration of minorities would have a telling effect on management, and (b) a firmly administered F.E.P.C. would tend to bolster community demands.

It cannot be said that such community demand had yet been greatly bolstered in Minneapolis, since the local Commission was handicapped financially. However, the ambivalent managerial attitude toward the employment of Negroes was an indifferent equilibrium, where legislation could move ahead of custom and thereby liberalize attitudes.

Undeserved

The above reasons for opposition to F.E.P.C. are oriented toward management welfare. Other respondents based their opposition on Negro welfare. One personnel manager claimed that Negroes do not deserve governmental assistance.

They've brought a lot of this on themselves. If they move into a new housing area, they let it deteriorate. One generation is no better than the previous one. They add nothing to the community, squander money on fancy cars and loud clothes, but don't spend any on keeping up homes or buying life insurance.

This manager was the only one who appealed to the middle-class value system.

Unnecessary

Four respondents said legislation is unnecessary. According to one, "the problem is very minor here because there are so few Negroes." Another

asked to be shown the evidence, because "discrimination is not flagrant."
A southern-born manager contended that "the law is entirely political,
designed simply to gain the votes of the Negroes." At greater length, another
blamed the whole situation on "agitators":

> A few self-seeking Negro leaders overemphasize the problem. There
> is no problem in Minnesota. It's just a question of agitators, out to
> make jobs for themselves in unions and other organizations.
> The law doesn't make any difference. There is no discrimination in
> Minneapolis. The ceiling is due to lack of training and education of the
> Negroes and to the habits of employers. If the Negro is qualified, he
> will get the job anyway. If he isn't qualified, the law makes no differ-
> ence.

The opinion that F.E.P.C. is unnecessary because the Twin Cities have
no discrimination is testable. The St. Paul Urban League published case
histories of trained Negroes who had left the Twin Cities or had been forced
to take menial jobs because of local discriminatory employment patterns.
The League reported that "27% of all the Negroes in St. Paul now engaged
in 'personal service jobs' such as porters and domestic servants are capable
of doing clerical and professional work."[8]

If the same percentage held true for my sample of stores, it would
mean that 21 janitors and scrubwomen were qualified for promotion not
simply to the semiskilled "other service" level but all the way to sales
and office positions. Presumably, still more Negroes working at the "other
service" level were capable of skilled work.

Boomerang Effects

By far the largest number of opposition arguments concerned with
Negro welfare predicted boomerang effects. Nine employers thought repercussions were likely, though none cited any bad effects that had been
actually observed in Minneapolis. "More ill feeling results from force. It
wouldn't benefit the Negro to be hired as a result of force." "The law
pushes change too fast." "There is too much attention to Negroes as a result of such laws." "It would accentuate race distinctions... [and] would
raise an issue already being achieved." The law "brings to a head an
irritation and tends to result in a defensive reaction on the part of the
employer." One manager warned that "you shouldn't force anything on
people. It's not good for the Negroes because it leads to resistance in the
whites." In the minds of these employers, the very people whom F.E.P.C.
is designed to help are hurt by it. If government does not interfere, the
race problem will be solved by fair-minded employers, once Negroes qualify
themselves for better positions. Meanwhile, the attempt to force the issue
through F.E.P.C. only delays the solution.

[8]St. Paul Urban League, "1949 Fact Sheet," 17th Vocational Opportunity Campaign,
March 13-20. (Mimeographed, two pages.)

Using a concept of "pluralistic ignorance," Krech and Crutchfield (1948) explain why boomerang reactions to governmental action do not always occur:

> ... The use of legal force, apparently against the wishes of many of the people in the community, *will occasionally not meet any significant resistance.* This is particularly true where a condition of "pluralistic ignorance" obtains. In some instances segregation practices *seem* to be supported by the beliefs and wishes of most of the people, but in actuality a condition exists where no one is in favor of segregation but everyone believes that everyone else is in favor of segregation. In such cases all that is needed is for someone or for a small minority to break through this apparent but non-existent resistance.

The Twin Cities retail situation involved pluralistic ignorance. Discrimination in employment rested not on managerial prejudice against Negroes but on the managers' assumptions of negative employee and customer reactions. In practice, those Twin Cities managers who introduced Negroes into skilled jobs encountered negligible resistance. Most managers were sympathetic to the employment of qualified persons regardless of race if that employment would not result in employee and customer repercussions. F.E.P.C. initiative was not likely to boomerang if accompanied by communication to employers of the facts about employee and customer acceptance in Minneapolis, New York, and elsewhere.

Not only does the preceding analysis contravene the prediction that fair-employment legislation heightens racial tension, but Robin Williams (1947) asserts that such legislation is likely to reduce tension.

> The existence of laws protecting the rights of minorities ... tends, in the long run, to decrease conflict over the rights involved. This result appears because of at least the following factors: (a) the set toward generalized conformity, resulting from the typical training of individuals in any social system; ... [and] (c) the presumption of legitimacy discourages conflict over rights claimed by minorities, by mobilizing intra-personality "conscience" functions of majority groups members.

We have already seen that few customers in New York or the Twin Cities resisted the *fait accompli* of a Negro salesgirl and that, similarly, few employees actively disputed management leadership. The same principles may be applied to the managers themselves; when they are faced with decisive leadership from a Fair Employment Practice Commission, few will resist.

Regional Differences

When asked about national legislation, 13 employers (including many who favored local action) spoke up on behalf of the South. Eight pointed out that the South has "special problems." Three confessed that they did not know enough about the South to support an F.E.P.C. law there. Whereas F.E.P.C. might work in the North, it was bound to fail south of the Mason-Dixon line. These men considered the southern color bar rigid and the southern white attitude so emotion-charged that government intervention would set off an explosion.

Four employers rejected federal action on the ground that fair employment is "not a proper field for federal legislation" but "should be decided locally." All four expressed a states-rights philosophy in one form or another.

The race problem is, of course, bigger and more complicated in the South than in the Twin Cities, but differences are of degree rather than kind. The South lags behind the North but the South, too, is changing. Southern employment opportunities widened considerably under the stimulus of the World War II labor shortage and the wartime F.E.P.C. As early as February 1943, manufacturing concerns and the wholesale and retail trades in the Deep South city of New Orleans were using Negroes in jobs where they had not been before (Wilson and Gilmore, 1943). And Arnold Rose (1949) evaluates the southern experience under F.E.P.C. as being far from disastrous.

> ... During the war, when we had a Federal F.E.P.C., most of the South adjusted itself quite reasonably to the employment of Negroes in factories. Negroes are still working in many new jobs opened by F.E.P.C. in the South—jobs from which they were barred before the war.

By 1964, Norgren and Hill could conclude their study of the trend toward fair employment with the assertion that

> ... extension of enforceable F.E.P.C. legislation beyond its present confines in the North and West will soon become a practicable possibility in several large Southern cities, in certain states in the upper South, and at the Federal government level.

Significantly, what Norgren and Hill mean by "practicable" refers to political possibility, not to enforceability in the South; enforceability they take for granted. The northern image of southern white reaction to F.E.P.C. is as fanciful as the parallel conception of negative employee and customer response to Negro salesgirls.

Better Ways

A number of employers volunteered suggestions for better ways of solving the race problem. The leading recommendation was education, which was proposed by five managers. One said, "Only education will change attitudes." Education of the American people generally and of employers in particular was advocated, with the newspapers and radio recommended as effective media. A southern-born manager stressed education of Negroes "to give them more skills."

Faith in "slow processes" was affirmed by two employers. The "constant work of churches and civic organizations" is more suitable than governmental action. Several respondents contended that stores should handle the problem without interference from outside agencies. One manager appealed to the law of supply and demand: "When there is a shortage of whites and some qualified Negroes come along, they'll get in. That's what happened in New York City; it wasn't due to the law there."

Only five respondents specifically advocated education instead of legislation, but the number would probably have been larger if all the alternatives to legislation had been listed in my questionnaire. Belief in education was shared by many Minnesota newspaper editors and by both political parties. Education was advocated in the 1948 platform of the Minnesota Republican party:

> We recognize the need for the establishment of a permanent Fair Employment Practices Commission ... at the same time realizing that only education can permanently eliminate the deep-seated emotional prejudices which are the cause of discrimination.[9]

This statement involves several inaccuracies. (1) There is little evidence from my research to substantiate the contention that "deep-seated emotional prejudices" are responsible for discrimination in employment. (2) Even where prejudiced attitudes exist, the attempt to change attitudes as a preliminary to changing discriminatory behavior involves a long and arduous detour. MacIver (1948) describes education as the long way around:

> Wherever the direct attack is feasible, i.e., the attack on discrimination itself, it is more promising than the indirect attack, that is the attack on prejudice as such. It is more effective to challenge conditions than to challenge attitudes or feelings.

Merton (1949) portrays education as at best a supplement to more drastic methods of social change:

> The appeal to "education" as a cure-all for the most varied social problems is rooted deep in the mores of America. Yet it is nonetheless illusory for all that. Education may serve as an operational adjunct but not as the chief basis for any but excruciatingly slow change in the prevailing patterns of race relations.

If the direct pressures of the Urban Leagues and other Twin Cities agencies were primarily responsible for the postwar employment breakthroughs, one may doubt that many gains would have been made if those organizations had confined their efforts to "education."

Education versus legislation is a false dichotomy. The Minneapolis law is educational when it gives Twin Cities employers the idea of hiring Negroes for better jobs. Drake and Cayton (1945) apply the same label to

[9]"Testimony in Support of the Minnesota F.E.P.C. Bill," p. 27.

direct-action methods used elsewhere to catapult Negroes into sales positions:

> Employers are educable—but such education in Chicago has included mass picket lines, petitions and protests, public hearings and legislation, as well as sweet reasonableness on the part of Negroes.

Maslow and Robison (1949) resolve the seeming contradiction between legislation and education.

> Legislation ... [is] one of the most, if not the most, effective procedures for achieving new conduct patterns. At the same time, *it has a direct educational effect.* Organized efforts to obtain legislation, even when they are unsuccessful, *teach* both the existence of discrimination and the necessity and feasibility of its elimination. Such education has a specific objective. It asks those to whom it is addressed to take concrete action. It is not cast in general terms of brotherhood which place no immediate demand on the individual. (Emphasis added.)

F.E.P.C. has an educational effect when first proposed, when passed, and throughout its existence:

> Again, the enactment and subsequent enforcement of antidiscrimination statutes continue the process of education. The activities of the enforcement agency are newsworthy events which tend to keep the problem before the public and to demonstrate that discrimination can be combatted successfully (Maslow and Robison, 1949).

Besides educating employers by provoking thought and providing examples of successful integration, F.E.P.C. has an educational effect on all participants, including managers, employees, and customers, in a store situation where F.E.P.C. spurs the introduction of a Negro salesgirl. Most northern whites have had little contact with skilled Negroes. When outside pressure places a Negro in a new job, whites have a chance to learn what a skilled, middle-class Negro is like.

> Perhaps the most potent weapon for attacking prejudice consists in making provision for natural contacts between groups of approximately the same social level in vocational or social situations where members of both pursue a common goal; the habit of cooperation is worth more than exhortation or argument because it focuses attention on areas of agreement rather than disagreement and allows understanding to proceed at its own pace (Schermerhorn, 1949).

Education, in the limited sense of the attempt to change attitudes through oral and written words, is tedious and restricted in effectiveness, though supplementally valuable. On the other hand, F.E.P.C. itself, far from being a mutually exclusive alternative, educates both by its sheer existence and by its activities. F.E.P.C. changes attitudes toward the employment of Negroes at skilled levels. Education is not a substitute for F.E.P.C. but one of its effects.

A second proffered alternative to F.E.P.C. was action by the stores them-selves. Although my respondents were thinking of individual action, a proposal had been made in St. Paul to tackle the problem jointly:

EMPLOYERS PLAN CURBS ON DISCRIMINATION
Hope to Eliminate Prejudice and End Need for Legislation
by Kenneth Crouse

St. Paul employers are seeking ways and means to eliminate, as far as possible, racial discrimination in the hiring and promotion of workers.

Spurred on by the narrow margin by which a fair employment prac-tices commission law was defeated in this year's Legislature, industry is attempting *to clean its own house* where necessary. It is a frank move to keep from giving F.E.P.C. sponsors any ammunition to use in the 1951 Legislature. The measure was killed in the last session by only a 33-to-28 vote in the Senate.

Several of the personnel men who testified against F.E.P.C. at legislative hearings are working on plans so industry can police itself on the discrimination issue. So far the plans are mostly in the discussion stage.

Employers as a whole realize that the weakness of F.E.P.C. proponents this year was that they did not have any sizable number of instances of discrimination to lay before the Legislature. Industry feels that mi-nority groups will be on the watch in the next two years in an effort to compile an imposing list of such cases. Therefore the move of business to police its own ranks.

One of the plans presently being discussed is to have a statewide employers' committee set up to which any person who felt he had been discriminated against could appeal. The committee would have no enforcement powers other than the pressure of other employers on the one involved in the case. That would be considerable.

Employers think there are few instances of actual discrimination be-cause of race. They take this view because business looks on employment as an economic proposition, wherein industry wants to employ the person on whom it can make the biggest profit.

Representatives of organized employers favor the appeals committee idea. Their chief fear is that such a committee might become a general employment agency for minority groups. This would defeat their idea, for the committee as presently conceived would be strictly a board of appeals.

In short, the plan would work like a voluntary F.E.P.C. only it would be operated entirely by employers.[10]

To managers opposed to F.E.P.C., this proposal is a logical approach to the problem of discrimination. Given belief in free enterprise, in the law of supply and demand, and in the good will of the average employer, an employers' appeal committee seems an attractive way of insuring justice to minority groups. According to Arnold Rose, employers in Cleve-land, Ohio tried a voluntary scheme for less than a year before admitting

[10]*The St. Paul Dispatch,* June 2, 1949.

that it did not work and requesting the City Council to pass a municipal F.E.P.C. ordinance. Despite the possibility of a similar sequence in St. Paul, the very concern of these personnel managers to police the ranks of industry and wipe out discriminatory hiring and promotion was itself an attempt to realize the aims of F.E.P.C., an attempt provoked by the introduction of an F.E.P.C. bill in the state legislature. This concern shows again how indirectly F.E.P.C. can affect the employment situation.

In a summary of managerial attitudes toward F.E.P.C., it should be emphasized that the arguments on both sides are essentially political. Most proponents argued that the American Creed demands a legislative solution to the problem of discrimination. Opponents were more apt to invoke supposedly "practical" obstacles, but sociological analysis removes most of those obstacles. What remains for the opposition is a conviction that the rights of management supercede Negro rights, that states' rights take priority over federal rights, and that slow evolution is better than rapid change. The choice between these views is a question of political philosophy.

Chapter 10

The Escalation of Conflict

In retrospect, the northern breakthroughs of the 1940s seem remarkably unexplosive. They occurred chiefly through behind-the-scenes case work. Negro candidates were interviewed one by one in Urban League and store offices. Store managers were visited one by one or quietly convened by Urban League officials for off-the-record meetings. And one by one, the managers experimented with their first white-collar Negroes.

When those experiments succeeded, they stimulated Negro demands for more jobs. To the managers, token employment was praiseworthy progress. To the Negro community, token employment proved that change was possible and that resistance could be overcome. With what the managers called "insatiable demands," the Negro agencies came back for more and more.

Change begets change. Token employment creates demands for full quotas. Breakthroughs at one job level create demands for still better jobs. Breakthroughs in one type of store stir thoughts about other types. Breakthroughs in retail stores increase eagerness for breakthroughs in other businesses. Once the wheels of employment progress begin to turn, they whirl faster and faster. And progress in employment creates demands for better housing, better schools, better recreational facilities.

Proliferation of Organizations

The first civil-rights group to engineer employment breakthroughs was the Urban League. But the League's specialization in job placement was a weakness as well as strength. As employment success created demands for progress on other fronts, the League was unable to lead the movement it had begun. The idea of desegregation had been kindled by the League, but that organization was too prosaic to become the vehicle for a mass movement.

The mantle passed to the N.A.A.C.P. Founded in 1909 (one year before the National Urban League), the National Association for the Advancement of Colored People established a Legal Defense Fund, which used lawsuits as a lever for changing the white establishment. This tool was effective against segregated southern public institutions. The N.A.A.C.P. was instrumental in securing the 1954 Supreme Court decision banning segregation in public schools and won decisions that opened public parks and libraries and desegregated interstate trains and buses.

The N.A.A.C.P. broadened the targets of the civil-rights movement from jobs to public facilities. But, try as it might, the N.A.A.C.P. was not a mass movement; it was too old, too successful, too middle-class, and too integrated for that.

Two organizations were not enough. If the economic and legal gains of the League and the N.A.A.C.P. were to spark a grass-roots movement, new organizations were needed. The masses needed to be organized. This task was the program of new organizations, C.O.R.E., S.C.L.C., and S.N.C.C.

The Congress of Racial Equality was founded in 1942 to apply non-violent, direct-action methods to the struggle for equality. Its Freedom Rides through the South implemented the "paper decision" on bus-station desegregation wrested from the Supreme Court by the N.A.A.C.P. (Lomax, 1962).

Though operating in the South, C.O.R.E. was initially a northern organization. Originating in the South was Martin Luther King's Southern Christian Leadership Conference. The Christian element in S.C.L.C. was an important innovation and has enabled this organization to mobilize Negro churches and their ministers into the civil-rights effort.

The Student Non-Violent Coordinating Committee ("Snick") was not a mass movement but contributed the talents of Negro and white students during college vacations, which often extended into drop-out years.

Other organizations will be formed in the future. The proliferation of organizations diversified the civil-rights movement. As a result, every Negro and every concerned white can find an organization to suit his taste and use his talents. The organizational smorgasbord may confuse the uninitiated, but it reaches a wider variety of people than any one organization could alone. Using different methods and working on different targets, multiple organizations achieve more than narrower approaches do. Even when aiming for the same target, multiple organizations are apt to mobilize greater pressure than could any one agency alone. Just as F.E.P.C. and the Urban League reinforced each other's efforts in Minneapolis, the subsequent proliferation of civil-rights organizations has made chain-reaction explosions of pressure more likely.

Escalation of Weaponry

One reason for the creation of new organizations is that people are dissatisfied with old methods. The trend is from conservative methods to radical ones, from casework and lawsuits to freedom rides and demonstrations. The escalation of weaponry occurs within organizations as well as between successive ones. Spurred by the success of young competitors, the N.A.A.C.P. became more activistic. C.O.R.E. and S.N.C.C. also evolved. Both these organizations were originally committed to nonviolence, as the "N" in S.N.C.C. suggests. C.O.R.E. was an offshoot of the Christian pacifist Fellowship of Reconciliation. Both initially applied the methods of Gandhi to the task of achieving inter-racial brotherhood. Both orginally had white junior leaders, members, and financial supporters.

In 1966, however, both organizations changed leaders and policies. The new slogan was "Black Power." It was the kind of slogan that had been used before only by extreme nationalists like the Black Muslims. The slogan suggested a go-it-alone movement of Negroes who intended to seize power from whites rather than to love them. Symptomatic of the shift was growing talk of Negro self-defense and even of militant aggression. White members and supporters of these organizations responded by resigning in large numbers. What began as a movement for integration of Negroes with whites and for assimilation into white American society threatened to become as segregationist and as racist as southern whites had ever been.[1]

From the 1940s to the 1960s, the weaponry of C.O.R.E. escalated from nonviolence to potential violence. In the streets of northern ghettoes, violence became more than potential. For Los Angeles, Detroit, and New York, "the long hot summer" became an ominous phrase. Negro men challenged by white policemen became the focal point of riot after riot. Rocks and Molotov cocktails hurled at police cars, at the cars of any whites, at white men's stores, and at any stores became the weapons of rage unleashed. Negro snipers fired at policemen and firemen. Terrified whites responded by exhausting retail stocks of rifles in Los Angeles and by intensified barrages of stones, garbage, and knives hurled at Negro demonstrators in Chicago. The movement for change escalated so far that it broke the bounds of organizational activity. The Negro masses, stirred from old lethargy, lashed out at their environment, and white masses lashed back.[2]

[1]This assertion is a controversial one. It refers to the tendency of "new left" spokesmen to question why anyone would want to be integrated into an American establishment devoted to the pursuit of international aggression and domestic profiteering. Given the mixed blessings of white America, it is easy to understand the temptation to romanticize the potential black contribution to a better world. It is also clear that there is great psychological appeal in the Black Power slogan. A segregationist Negro strategy may even be a necessary means to the goal of integration. I reiterate, however, that the ultimate goal must be an integrated society if race prejudice and discrimination are to disappear and that even strategic segregation cannot be practiced without incurring losses that at least partially offset whatever gains may accrue.

[2]Since my concern is to trace the history of the civil-rights movement, I have focused on changes in Negro tactics. The white backlash was not the first occasion when violence had been used against Negroes. The long history of Negro lynchings is all too familiar. John Leggett points out that, even in the midst of the 1965 Watts riot, it

The Impetus to Escalation

What caused this conflict between Negroes and whites to escalate? Escalation is a self-generating process. We have slogans for it: "Nothing succeeds like success." Early gains whet the appetite for further gains and create a "revolution of rising expectations." The trouble is that gains never come fast enough to keep up with escalating expectations. When expectations rise faster than actualities, the gap between them widens, even though conditions may improve objectively. The net result is that grievances escalate, too. Conditions taken for granted a decade before now seem unbearable. Goals that seemed impossibly distant a generation before now become imperative.[3]

The faster concessions are won, the less the impetus to escalate. But concessions always lag, wrung one by one from reluctant whites. So the impetus is always there. As indignation rises, old methods seem too slow. As hate flares, nonviolence seems too good for the whites. As poorer Negroes are mobilized, the movement fills with men with no talent for delicate negotiation but who know how to use their fists. Escalation, then, is inevitable until the struggle becomes so successful that Negroes have more to lose than to gain by prolonging the battle.

The Consequences of Escalation

I have already suggested that escalating the conflict between Negroes and whites may threaten the goal of integration. When Negro-white hostility intensifies enough, neither race wants to have anything to do with the other.

Nationalism was useful to colored nations controlled by imperial powers. They could throw off white rule and become independent nations. But American Negroes have no such future.[4] The only solution to race preju-

was mostly Negroes who got clobbered—the death toll: one white, 32 Negroes. Moreover, in the South, almost all the casualties of the civil-rights struggle have been Negroes.

[3]To the self-generating character of any revolutionary movement must be added the peculiar historical circumstances of the mid-1960s. President Lyndon B. Johnson launched his War on Poverty amid great fanfare as one of his chief means for achieving the Great Society. This program raised new hopes in the Negro ghettoes, only to lead to new frustrations when the War on Poverty became one of the casualties of that other war in Vietnam. John Leggett suggests that, even if Vietnam had not intervened, the domestic program was "doomed from the very beginning by lack of funds plus local political interference (mounted by the community Democratic party organization in cities such as New York, Chicago, San Francisco, and Los Angeles)."

[4]Throughout the years, some Negroes have advocated secession. For example, some proposed the establishment of a black nation carved out of the Black Belt of Alabama and Mississippi. The trouble with such proposals is that Negroes are too small a fraction of the American body politic to be able to secede any more successfully than the whole South could in 1861. Moreover, the migration of Negroes out of the Black

dice in American society is integration. And "Black Power" is hardly an integrative slogan.

Ultimately there must be de-escalation and disarmament. No peace treaty will mark the end of the war, but Negroes will eventually win access to every corner of American society, and the conflict will peter out. Nor will the war end simultaneously on every front. Rather, as the luckiest Negroes are inducted into the middle class, they will be lost to the cause. Although the earliest gains may escalate the conflict, the ultimate ones lead the beneficiaries to abandon the struggle. Black solidarity is possible only as long as all blacks are in the same situation. Those who escape from the ghetto into the suburbs, from ditch-digging into the professions, from poverty into affluence, find their enthusiasm for picketing cooled. Just as white liberals seldom maintain as much dedication to the cause as poor blacks, who feel directly involved in it, so rich black men will gradually opt out of the conflict.

In the meantime, does escalation make matters better or worse? Does intensified conflict contribute anything to the achievement of integration?[5] The mobilization of Negroes was necessary not simply to intensify pressure on whites but to create hope, to raise aspirations, and thereby to persuade Negroes to take advantage of the opportunities that organized pressure had won for them.

(1) White complacency has been shattered. No one can say anymore that Negroes are satisfied with their lot.

(2) Negro apathy has been shattered. White complacency was possible as long as Negroes accepted their situation fatalistically. The escalation of the Negro revolt shook Negroes free of that fatalism.

(3) Government responded to the threats to "domestic peace and tranquility" that came with escalated racial conflict. Congress passed civil-rights bills so regularly that they came to be known as "The Civil Rights Bill of 1965," and so on. Northern cities and states passed laws in advance of the Federal Government. In 1965, eight more states passed fair-employment-practice laws, bringing the total to 32.

Belt into the urban ghettoes has scattered them too widely to be able to put the pieces back together again.

Others believe that American Negroes have more in common with the colored nations of the world than with white America, so they should join in a common "class-racial struggle" against the powers that be. This argument seems unlikely to appeal to more than a tiny minority of American Negroes. Their colored brothers are too far away geographically, too hard to understand linguistically, and too far beneath them economically to be easily identified with. For better or for worse, most American Negroes are destined to conceive of themselves as primarily Americans rather than as colored world citizens.

[5] For an analysis of the role of demonstrations and other activist tactics of the civil-rights movement, see Arthur I. Waskow, " 'Creative Disorder' in the Racial Struggle," in Murphy and Elinson (1966).

(4) Laws and court decisions that might once have been worthless were more apt to be enforced by governments panicked into doing something.

When the dust settles and the revolution is over, Americans will be able to look back and say, "It all began so unobtrusively with a breakthrough here and a breakthrough there. . . ."

Appendix A

Research Methods

Selection of the Stores

I needed lists of the stores in each city that employed the largest number of people. Since no official employment statistics were available, the following method of selection was used.

The retail secretary of the St. Paul Association of Commerce checked on his membership list the 21 largest stores. In only one case did revision prove necessary. One store had a diminutive retail force and a large factory force for the manufacture of fur coats. Because the official had failed to separate the two types of employment, this store was dropped and a substitute recommended by a St. Paul official of the Minnesota Employment Service.

Because Minneapolis is bigger than St. Paul, I decided that the number of stores covered should be correspondingly larger, namely 30. The Minneapolis Chamber of Commerce, however, had no retail membership section, so the official had more difficulty preparing a list of the largest stores. His list of 30 included many small fur and jewelry stores of the "exclusive" variety and failed to include 12 stores suggested by the Minneapolis Urban League and the Joint Committee on Employment Opportunity. Hence, a scrambled list of 42 stores was presented to a research officer of the Minnesota Employment Service in Minneapolis who was familiar with the local retail situation. He discarded the 12 smallest stores. In order to avoid bias in selection, neither the Chamber of Commerce nor the Employment Service official was told the purpose of my inquiry.

The Stores

I studied 50 stores (omitting one refusal)—29 in Minneapolis, and 21 in St. Paul. The total number of full-time employees in the Minneapolis stores was 11,734. This number was 33.5% of the total number of full-time employees in retail trade in Minneapolis in 1948. Coverage in St. Paul was slightly smaller: 5,829, or 30.6%.[1] Since the study excluded all food stores,

[1]United States Bureau of the Census, *Census of Business*, "Retail Trade—Area Statistics," III (1948), 22.07, 22.09.

a substantial proportion of the remaining retail trade of each city was covered.

Since I included more of the total retail labor force in Minneapolis, the study also reached into smaller stores there. Six Minneapolis stores had less than 50 employees, and the smallest had but 20, whereas in St. Paul the only store with less than 50 had 31. That Minneapolis has more large stores than St. Paul offsets this difference.

Median sizes for the two cities are fairly close. The median store studied in Minneapolis had 127 employees, in St. Paul 134. By size of sales force alone, the typical stores in the two cities had 50 and 64 clerks, respectively. In both cities the median number of Negroes for stores employing any Negroes was five.

Most department stores and some specialized stores in both cities are old institutions with long traditions. Eight St. Paul stores and nine Minneapolis stores were established before 1900. Many of the newer stores (especially the variety, clothing, and drug stores) belong to chains. Yet almost all stores, whether locally owned or not, claim freedom to choose their employees as they see fit. Only five managers said they would consult chain headquarters before venturing to hire a Negro salesgirl or office worker.

One of these five managers complained that "chains are apt to be criticized for doing anything new" and indicated that he would feel freer to pioneer if he owned the store himself. Another manager, personally quite liberal, said he would want to be sure of home-office approval: "It's always good policy to ask questions beforehand—then you can't be criticized afterwards."

Although the stores were not selected on a stratified basis, approximately the same types of stores are represented in the two cities (see Table A-1).

Table A-1
Types of Stores Studied, by City

TYPE OF STORE	MINNEAPOLIS		ST. PAUL	
Department stores		31%		33%
Clothing		28		34
women's	17%		19%	
men's and women's	4		10	
men's	7		5	
Furniture		17		14
Variety stores		4		14
Drug stores		10		0
Hardware		10		0
Stationery		0		5
Total		100%		100%
Number of stores		29		21

We may conclude that the stores in the two cities are roughly comparable according to many external indices. This similarity makes the comparisons made in this study more valid.

The Interview Schedule

The interview schedule reflects the advice of Professors Neal Gross and Theodore Caplow, of Frank Fager of the Mayor's Council on Human Relations (Minneapolis), and the results of a pretest with a personnel officer of a large department store.

1. Name of firm_____Phone_____

2. Address _____
                 Street   City

3. Date and hour of interview_____._____

4. Interviewee _____
                    Name   Title

5. What year did this company begin operation?_____

6. Is personnel policy determined locally_____or elsewhere?_____

7. How many employees do you have altogether?_____

8. Can you tell me approximately how many are employed in each of the job classifications on the printed card?
   (a) Janitorial (porters, matrons, maids, etc.)_____
   (b) Other service (elevator, stock room, maintenance, etc.)_____
   (c) Sales personnel_____
   (d) Clerical_____
   (e) Executive_____

9. Do you have any Negro employees? Yes:_____No:_____

10. Do you know how many you have altogether?_____

11. Can you tell me approximately how many are employed in each of those same five job classifications?_____
    (If none now but some previously, list in parentheses the maximum number employed at any one time, e.g. (1). (See blanks below.)

12. Do you know when your company hired the first Negro in each classification?

13. Have any Negroes ever applied for jobs in any other classifications (i.e., other than those in which they have been hired)?

	11. Number	12. Date first hired	13. Others applied
(a) Janitorial	_____	_____	_____
(b) Other service	_____	_____	_____
(c) Sales personnel	_____	_____	_____
(d) Clerical	_____	_____	_____
(e) Executive	_____	_____	_____

14. Does your company keep special records on Negroes? Yes:____ No:____

15. How did you happen to employ the first Negro in a sales position? (s)
    How did you happen to employ the first Negro in a clerical position? (c)
OR What factors (if any) are leading you to consider the possibility of employing Negroes in sales positions? And/or in clerical positions?
    (If more than one factor, number in order of importance.)

(a) First applicant. s:_____c:_____
(b) An executive. s:_____c:_____ Which?
(c) Other employer. s:_____c:_____ Where?
(d) No whites available. s:_____c:_____
(e) Urban League. s:_____c:_____ How?
(f) Self-Survey. s:_____c:_____ How?
(g) Joint Committee on Employment Opportunity. s:_____c:_____
       How?
(h) F.E.P.C. s:_____c:_____ How?
(i) Other (specify). s:_____c:_____
Do you have any further comments?

16. What has been the quality of the work done by your Negro sales per-
    sonnel? By your clerical personnel?
OR If local Negroes were to be employed as sales personnel by your com-
    pany, what do you think would be the quality of their work?
    If local Negroes were to be employed as clerical personnel by your com-
    pany, what do you think would be the quality of their work?

(a) Experience			(b) Prediction	
sales	clerical		sales	clerical
_____	_____	very satisfactory	_____	_____
_____	_____	satisfactory	_____	_____
_____	_____	mixed	_____	_____
_____	_____	unsatisfactory	_____	_____
_____	_____	very unsatisfactory	_____	_____

Specifically:

Did they do much better_____better_____the same_____worse_____or
much worse_____than you expected? (Mark with s or c.)
Specifically:

17. How have your other employees reacted to your employment of Negro
    sales personnel?
OR How do you think your other employees would react to the employment
    of Negro sales personnel?

What reaction had you expected from your employees?

(b) How have your other employees reacted to your employment of
       Negro clerical personnel?
OR   How do you think your other employees would react to the em-
       ployment of Negro clerical personnel?

What reaction had you expected from your employees?

18. What customer reactions to the employment of Negro sales personnel have come to your attention?
OR What reactions of your customers to the employment of Negro sales personnel do you think would come to your attention?

What reaction had you expected from your customers?

19. How do you personally feel about the passage of legislation against discrimination in employment?

	About Minneapolis ordinance?		About ordinance for St. Paul?	About a law for Minnesota?	About a U.S. F.E.P.C.?
	(a) Now (1949)	(b) Before adopted in 1947			
Strongly and publicly support	_____	_____	_____	_____	_____
Support	_____	_____	_____	_____	_____
Neutral	_____	_____	_____	_____	_____
Oppose	_____	_____	_____	_____	_____
Strongly and publicly oppose	_____	_____	_____	_____	_____
Don't know enough to say	_____	_____	_____	_____	_____

Reasons?

What is the company policy on this?

20. Is there anything else you think I ought to know about this subject?

21. (Optional) In order to check on the reliability of my interviewing, is there someone else here I could talk to also?

The scale of job classifications is an original one, since those used by Drake and Cayton (1945) and in the Minnesota Occupational Classification were inappropriate. Sales, clerical, and executive personnel are self-explanatory. Other retail employees are normally categorized as the "supporting services." However, because Negroes have been traditionally assigned to janitorial jobs, supporting services were split in order to reveal how many Twin Cities Negroes were so limited in their work assignments. The check list of job classifications was typed onto a separate card given to the respondent to aid in answering questions 8, 11, 12, and 13. If individual

Negroes performed both janitorial and stock-room functions, they were listed in the higher category as "other service" personnel.

The schedule lists the answers to question 15 in abbreviated form. As given to the respondent on a second card, the full answers (in the form appropriate to Minneapolis) were as follows:

(a) Qualified Negro applying for such a position for the first time.
(b) Initiative of a company executive.
(c) Favorable experience of other employer.
(d) No qualified white available for the position.
(e) The Minneapolis Urban League.
(f) The Community Self-Survey.
(g) Joint Committee on Employment Opportunity.
(h) Minneapolis F.E.P.C. Ordinance (Fair Employment Practice Commission).
(i) Other (please specify).

For the St. Paul respondents, the Community Self-Survey, the Joint Committee on Employment Opportunity, and the F.E.P.C. Ordinance were omitted as inapplicable, and the card listed the St. Paul instead of the Minneapolis Urban League.

In question 19, the respondent was asked his attitude toward a local F.E.P.C. ordinance for his own city only, not for both cities.

Securing the Interviews

On the advice of the industrial secretary of the Minneapolis Urban League, the personnel managers, rather than the store managers, were the officials interviewed whenever possible, as the former are in closer contact with the routine employment policies and experiences of their companies.

Interviews were secured in August 1949. Typical interviews required 20 minutes to half an hour, although occasional loquacious managers talked extensively after the interview schedule was completed.

Only one store refused to provide an interview. Advance arrangements had been made with the manager by telephone, but when contacted in person on the floor of the store, he expressed hesitancy about giving up 20 minutes. After looking at the schedule, he suggested that the district personnel manager could answer the questions better. The latter, however, knew nothing about the policies of local stores because "each store is run independently by its own manager." Moreover, he said, "If I were the manager of that store, I would be very reluctant to tell you how many employees I had because then all my competitors would know how much business I was doing. However, why don't you see the assistant district manager—he'll be back in the office tomorrow."

I assured him that the number of employees in the local store would be divulged to no one. None of the 50 stores already contacted had expressed any anxiety about reporting the number of their employees. But he was not impressed.

One more attempt was made to interview the local store manager, only to be told that, since the district personnel manager had specified seeing the assistant district manager, no questions would be answered. Apparently the district personnel manager had telephoned the local manager his instructions.

The following day, a friend of mine telephoned the assistant district manager:

> He was very congenial. He said that he would make an appointment for me at 3 o'clock with the district personnel manager. When I arrived at 3 o'clock, the district personnel manager was gone for the day, and the assistant district manager wasn't seeing anyone. So I got absolutely nowhere.

In a furtive conversation, a sympathetic employee of the company's district office confided that there had been trouble with the F.E.P.C. because of the failure of the Minneapolis store to hire Negroes. This statement illuminates the resistance encountered.

By contrast, no difficulty was experienced in interviewing an official in the St. Paul outlet of the same chain. Even more significantly, the "Bulletin of the Joint Committee for Employment Opportunity," dated May 24, 1949, states that the Minneapolis store is one of the few that have employed Negro salesgirls. Such stores usually grant interviews freely because they are proud of their liberality.

Carrying Out the Interviews

The privacy of the respondent's office was preferred for the interview in order to keep social pressure at a minimum.[2] The usual procedure was to read the questions to the respondent in the form and sequence of the mimeographed schedule. Frequently, however, a respondent would ask for amplification of the meaning of a question. And sometimes the respondent's chain of association led him to comment about events and opinions that had to be recorded in various parts of the schedule.

Occasionally, the controversial implications of the questions strained relationships between the respondent and me. One store owner began to balk halfway through the schedule; he protested that "there is an overemphasis on race and color in this questionnaire. This isn't an employment study but a racial survey. I wouldn't have granted the interview if I had known what it is about, because it puts me on the spot." Fortunately, his was an extreme case.

---

[2] I had feared lest news of, and opposition to, the survey might travel from store to store, but this seems never to have occurred.

By contrast, the two Southerners interviewed were cordial and cooperative. One wanted my opinion on many related matters after the schedule
was completed. Perhaps the Southerners felt comfortable with their prejudices, whereas the tense Northerner found himself accused by his own
ideals.

The Use of Rechecks

Rechecking was used once in each city. In Minneapolis, interviewing a
second personnel officer of the same store showed wide discrepancies in
the breakdown of job classifications (question 8). One said "yes" and the
other "no" to the question on whether Negroes had ever applied for
clerical jobs. One mentioned top management, the Urban League, and the
F.E.P.C. as responsible for the decision to employ Negro salesgirls, whereas
the other checked none of these factors and mentioned simply "the evolution
of public opinion." One favored and the other opposed the Minneapolis
F.E.P.C. law.

Two personnel officers of a St. Paul store disagreed even more sharply.
Not only did they report different numbers of total employees (of all
races) in each category, but one forgot to mention the five Negro matrons
employed by the store. The officers disagreed about whether Negroes were
being considered for clerical work. One listed the store's experience with
Negro sales personnel as "very unsatisfactory" and "much worse than had
been expected," whereas the other interpreted that same work as "mixed"
in quality and, on the whole, the same as had been expected (at first,
"much better" than expected). One found the reaction of white employees
"the same as expected," while the other judged it "better than expected."
The first mentioned negative as well as positive customer comments, whereas
the second knew of only favorable responses.

These rechecks show how widely individuals can differ about the same
phenomena. The evaluation of the work done by a single salesgirl varies
strikingly according to the propensities of the official. If he is sympathetic to Negroes, he will put the best possible interpretation on what may
appear to be a relatively poor performance. If, on the other hand, low
sales confirm deep-seated prejudices, the manager will evaluate the situation
quite differently.

Presumably, the number of stores included in this study is large enough
to cover the range of managerial opinions and to avoid the bias that might
come from an unrepresentative, small sample.

Appendix B

Early State and Municipal Fair-Employment-Practice Laws

	N.Y. '45	MASS. '46	CONN. '47	CHI. '45	MPLS. '47	PHIL. '48
SUBJECT TO ACT:						
1. All enterprises conducted for profit	x	x	x	x	x	x
2. Labor organizations	x	x	x		x	x
3. Employment agencies	x	x	x			x
4. Government agencies	x	x	x	x	x	x
EXCLUDED:						
1. Nonprofit enterprises	x	x	x			x
2. Employers of less than	6	6	6		2	1
3. Domestic and family employees	x	x	x			x
ILLEGAL PRACTICES:						
1. Discrimination by employers in hiring, firing, or working conditions	x	x	x	x	x	x
2. Discrimination by labor organizations in the right to or privileges of membership	x	x	x		x	x
3. Advertisements specifying or inquiries concerning race, creed, or national origin of applicants for jobs	x	x	x	x	x	x
4. Refusal of employees to work with minority-group members	x					x
5. Discrimination against persons filing complaints under the act	x	x	x			x
6. Failure to post notices of the act		x				
7. Aiding or inciting violation of the act	x	x	x			x
MAXIMUM PENALTIES FOR VIOLATIONS:						
1. 1 yr. or $500	x	x				
2. $200				x		
3. 90 days or $100					x	
4. 30 days or $100						x
ADMINISTERED BY:						
1. Separate commission	x	x	x		x	x
SALARY (thousands per yr.):						
1. Chairman	10	5				
2. Members	10	4				
POWERS OF COMMISSION:						
1. Receive and investigate complaints	x	x	x		x	x
2. Initiate complaints		x	x			x
3. Maintain offices	x	x	x		x	x
4. Meet and function at any point in the state	x	x				
5. Appoint staff	x	x	x			
6. Conciliation	x	x	x			x
7. Subpoena witnesses	x	x	x			x
8. Conduct hearings	x	x	x		x	x
9. Issue cease-and-desist orders	x	x	x			
10. Create advisory councils	x	x				

11. Issue publications	x	x			x	
REVIEW AND ENFORCEMENT:						
1. Judicial	x	x	x			x
APPROPRIATIONS:						
(Thousands per year)	372	55	54			

Source: Compilation by Professor Theodore Caplow. The 1945 New Jersey law is not included.

Appendix C

The Minneapolis F.E.P.C. Ordinance, as Amended October 29, 1948: An Ordinance

To Prohibit Discriminatory Practices in employment and in membership in labor unions based upon Race, Color, Creed, National Origin, or Ancestry; to Create a Commission on Job Discrimination, Prescribing its Duties and Powers; and for other Purposes; and Providing Penalties for Violations thereof.

The Council of the City of Minneapolis does hereby ordain:

Section 1 FINDINGS AND DECLARATION OF POLICY

(a) Discrimination in public and private employment on the grounds of race, creed, color, national origin, or ancestry, with consequent arbitrary denial of job opportunities to large groups of inhabitants of this City, foments strife, creates unrest, disturbances, disorders and group tensions, and substantially and adversely affects the general welfare and good order of this City.

(b) Such job discrimination tends unjustly to condemn large groups of inhabitants of this City to depressed living conditions, which breed vice, ignorance, disease, degeneration, juvenile delinquency and crime, thereby causing grave injury to the public safety, general welfare and good order of this City, and endangering the public health thereof.

(c) Such job discrimination and the resulting effects on the community and the inhabitants thereof tend to impose substantial financial burdens on the public revenues for the relief and amelioration of conditions so created.

(d) Experience has proved that legislative enactment prohibiting such job discrimination removes some of the sources of strife, unrest, poverty, disease, juvenile delinquency and crime, and would directly promote the general welfare and good order of this City.

(e) The right of every inhabitant of this City to job opportunities without being subjected to such job discrimination is hereby declared to be a civil right.

(f) This Ordinance shall be deemed an exercise of the police power of this City, for the protection of the public welfare and the health and peace of the inhabitants thereof.

Section 2 DEFINITIONS

(a) The word "discriminate," "discriminates," or "discrimination" wherever used in this Ordinance, is hereby defined and declared to mean and include discrimination on the ground or because of race, creed, color, national origin or ancestry.

(b) The word "employee" wherever used in this Ordinance is hereby defined and declared not to include an employee in domestic service, or an employee of an organized religious congregation or an institution limited in its membership to persons of a single religious faith.

(c) The word "employer" wherever used in this Ordinance is hereby defined and declared to include only employers of two or more employees within the City of Minneapolis.

Section 3

It shall be unlawful for any head of department, official, or agent or employee of the City of Minneapolis, or of any department thereof, acting for or on behalf of said City, in any manner involving employment by said City, to discriminate against any person otherwise qualified, in employment or in tenure, terms or conditions of employment; or to discriminate in promotion or increase in compensation; or to publish offers of or to offer employment based upon such discrimination; or to adopt or enforce any rule or employment policy which discriminates between employees or prospective employees; or to seek information relative to race, creed, color, national origin or ancestry from any person or any employee, as a condition of employment tenure, terms, or in connection with conditions of employment, promotion or increase in compensation; or to discriminate in the selection of personnel for training.

Section 4

Said City and all of its contracting agencies and departments thereof shall include in all contracts hereafter negotiated, a provision obligating the contractor not to discriminate against any employee of, or applicant for employment with, such contractor in the City of Minneapolis, and shall require such contractors to include a similar provision in all sub-contracts to be performed in the City of Minneapolis.

Section 5

(a) It shall be unlawful for any employer within said City to discriminate against any person in connection with any hiring, application for employment, tenure, terms or conditions of employment.

(b) It shall be unlawful for any person, firm or corporation engaged in the business of or acting as an employment, referral or vocational placement agency or bureau within said City, to discriminate against any person in connection with any application for employment, referral for employment, hiring, tenure, terms or conditions of employment.

(c) It shall be unlawful for any employer covered by this Ordinance or labor union or any person, firm or corporation engaged in the business of or acting as an employment, referral or vocational placement agency or bureau with respect to employees covered by this Ordinance within said City to include in an application form or biographical statement relating to employment any questions or statements designed to elicit or record information concerning the race, creed, color, national origin or ancestry of the applicant.

Section 6

It shall be unlawful for any labor union within said City to discriminate against any person with respect to membership in said labor union.

Section 7

There is hereby created a permanent Commission on Job Discrimination, which shall consist of a chairman and four other members, to be appointed by the Mayor and to be confirmed by the City Council. The first chairman shall be appointed for a term of five years, and the remaining four members shall be first appointed for terms respectively of four years, three years, two years, and one year. Each of said appointees shall serve for his respective term and until his respective successor has been appointed, and has assumed office. After the expiration of the initial term, each of the members shall be appointed and shall serve for a five-year term, and until his respective successor has been appointed, and has assumed office. They shall serve without compensation. Said Committee shall be charged with the duties of:

(a) Effectuating the purpose and policies of this Ordinance.

(b) Receiving complaints of violations of this Ordinance, and investigating into the merits thereof.

(c) Promoting cooperation among all groups for the purpose of effectuating the purposes and policies of this Ordinance.

(d) Conducting studies, surveys, and projects and disseminating information concerning job discrimination and related problems.

(e) Aiding in the enforcement of this Ordinance.

(f) Make reports of its activities to the City Council annually or more often, as requested by said City Council.

The Commission shall hear all complaints on violations and shall after said hearing certify and recommend to the City Attorney for prosecution those complaints which in the judgement of said Commission are deemed to be violations of this Ordinance.

Nothing in this section contained shall be construed to limit the right of a complainant to make and file a complaint without such certificate or recommendation by said Commission.

Section 8

Any person, whether acting in an official capacity, or in a private capacity, who shall violate or fail to comply with any of the provisions of this Ordinance shall be guilty of a misdemeanor, and shall be punished by fine not exceeding $100.00 or by imprisonment in the workhouse for a period of not to exceed ninety (90) days.

Section 9

If any provisions of this Ordinance or the application of such provision to any person or circumstance shall be held invalid, the remainder of such Ordinance or the application of such provision to persons or circumstances other than those to which it has been held invalid shall not be affected thereby.

Section 10

This Ordinance shall be in force and effect from and after its publication.

(Note: This Minneapolis Fair Employment Practice Ordinance was originally passed by the Minneapolis City Council by a vote of 21 to three on January 31, 1947. The ordinance was published and put into effect on February 5, 1947.)

References

Brink, William, and Louis Harris. *The Negro Revolution in America*. New York: Simon and Schuster, 1963.

Brophy, Ira N. "The Luxury of Anti-Negro Prejudice," *Public Opinion Quarterly*, IX (1946), 456–466.

Dean, John P., and Alex Rosen. *A Manual of Intergroup Relations*. Chicago: University of Chicago Press, 1955.

Drake, St. Clair, and Horace R. Cayton. *Black Metropolis: A Study of Negro Life in a Northern City*. New York: Harcourt, Brace & World, 1945.

Fowler, Albert V. "Philadelphia Likes the F.E.P.C. Idea," *The Progressive* (April 1950), pp. 23–24.

Frazier, E. Franklin. *The Negro in the United States*. New York: Macmillan Co., 1949.

Governor's Inter-racial Commission of Minnesota. *The Negro Worker in Minnesota: a report to Governor Edward J. Thye*. St. Paul, 1945.

Greenberg, Jack. *Race Relations and American Law*. New York: Columbia University Press, 1959.

Haas, F. J., and G. J. Fleming. "Personnel Practices and War-Time Changes," *The Annals of the American Academy of Political and Social Science*, CCXLIV (1946), 48–56.

Johnson, Charles S. *The Negro in American Civilization*. New York: Holt, Rinehart and Winston, 1930.

——————. *Patterns of Negro Segregation*. New York: Harper & Row, Publishers, 1943.

Kohn, Melvin L., and Robin M. Williams, Jr. "Situational Patterning in Intergroup Relations," *American Sociological Review*, XXI (1956), 164–174.

Krech, David, and Richard S. Crutchfield. *Theory and Problems of Social Psychology*. New York: McGraw-Hill Book Co., 1948.

Lenski, Gerhard E. "Status Crystallization: A Non-Vertical Dimension of Social Status," *American Sociological Review*, XIX (1954), 405–413.

Lewin, Kurt. "Research on Minority Problems," *Technology Review*, XLVIII (1946), 163–4, 182–190.

Lomax, Louis E. *The Negro Revolt*. New York: Harper & Row, Publishers, 1962.

MacIver, Robert M. *The More Perfect Union*. New York: Macmillan Co., 1948.

Maslow, Will. "The Law and Race Relations," *Annals of the American Academy of Political and Social Science*, CCXLIV (1946), 75–81.

Maslow, Will, and Joseph B. Robison. "Legislating Against Discrimination," *Social Action*, XV (1949), 4–26.

Merton, Robert K. *Social Theory and Social Structure*. New York: The Free Press, 1949.

——————. "Discrimination and the American Creed," in Robert M. MacIver, ed., *Discrimination and National Welfare*. New York: Harper & Row, Publishers, 1949a.

Murphy, Raymond J., and Howard Elinson, eds. *Problems and Prospects of the Negro Movement*. Belmont, Calif.: Wadsworth Publishing Co., 1966.

Myrdal, Gunnar. *An American Dilemma: The Negro Problem and Modern Democracy*. New York: Harper & Row, Publishers, 1944.

Noland, E. William, and E. Wight Bakke. *Workers Wanted*. New York: Harper & Row, Publishers, 1949.

Norgren, Paul H., Albert N. Webster, Roger D. Borgeson, and Maud B. Patten. *Employing the Negro in American Industry: A Study of Management Practices*. New York: Industrial Relations Counselors, Inc., 1959.

Norgren, Paul H., and Samuel E. Hill. *Toward Fair Employment*. New York: Columbia University Press, 1964.

O'Connor, William B. "The Use of Colored Persons in Skilled Occupations," *The Conference Board Management Record* (December 1941), pp. 156–158.

Parsons, Talcott, and Kenneth B. Clark. *The Negro American*. Boston: Houghton Mifflin Co., 1966.

Pettigrew, Thomas F. "Complexity and Change in American Racial Patterns: A Social Psychological View," in Parsons and Clark, *The Negro American*, pp. 325–359.

Rose, Arnold. "A New Noose for Negroes," *The Progressive* (September 1949), pp. 10–12.

Saenger, Gerhart, and Emily Gilbert. "Customer Reactions to the Integration of Negro Sales Personnel," *International Journal of Opinion and Attitude Research*, IV (1950), 57–76.

Schermerhorn, Richard A. *These Our People: Minorities in American Culture*. Boston: D.C. Heath & Co., 1949.

Sheatsley, Paul B. "White Attitudes toward the Negro," in Parsons and Clark, *The Negro American*, pp. 302–324.

Stouffer, Samuel A., and others. *The American Soldier, I. Adjustment to Army Life*. Princeton: Princeton University Press, 1949.

Index

American Creed, 62, 63, 67–68, 74, 117
American Federation of Labor (A.F.L.), hiring of Negroes, 43
Army, Negro-white relations in, 40–41, 46–47, 70, 72
Augsburg College study of customer reaction, 59

"Black Power," 133
Boston, effect of F.E.P.C. law, 118, 120
Breakthroughs:
  in clerical work, 36–39
  domino theory, 108–109
  in established vs. new stores, 85–86
  in Jewish vs. Gentile stores, 83–85
  in large vs. small stores, 86–87
  managerial readiness for, 80–87
  pressure groups, 88–111 (see also Pressure groups)
  in sales, 25–36
  timetable, 6–9

Chicago:
  customer reaction in, 73
  employment picture in, 11, 23–24
Civil-rights movement:
  beginnings of, 3
  "Black Power," 133
  Congress of Racial Equality (C.O.R.E.), 132, 133
  escalation of, 131–136
  National Association for the Advancement of Colored People (N.A.A.C.P.), 131–132, 133
  new tactics, 132–133

Civil-rights movement: (continued)
  organizations involved in, 131–132
  Southern Christian Leadership Conference (S.C.L.C.), 132
  Student Non-Violent Coordinating Committee (S.N.C.C.), 132, 133
  Urban League, 131 (see also Urban League)
  white backlash, 133, 133n
Clerical work, 16, 18–19, 20–21, 49–52, 79, 108–109
  breakthrough vs. sales breakthrough, 38–39
  evaluation of performance, 36–39
  proportion of Negroes in, 11–21
Clothing stores, 19–20, 31–32, 83, 86
Community Self-Survey of Human Relations, 88, 98
Congress of Racial Equality (C.O.R.E.), 132, 133
Customer reactions, 53–60, 73
  actual, 56–60
  predicted, 53–56
  by religious affiliation, 59–60
  of southern-born customers, 55, 57

Department stores, employment picture, 17, 18–19, 21–24, 86 (see also Negro clerical workers, Negro sales clerks)
Discipline problems, 26–28, 32
Discrimination, 10–21, 61–75 (see also Job ceiling, Liberalism)
  causes, 68–73
  without prejudice, 68–73
  public vs. private, 67–68
  tokenism, 10, 21–24

153

Urban League (continued)
    underemployment, 5n, 8, 24
    as placement and screening
        agency, 6, 25, 94–96
    use of propaganda, 92–94
    on token employment, 21
    as troubleshooter, 27–28, 95

White backlash, 133, 133–134n
Whites:
    office workers, reactions to
        breakthrough, 49–52
    salesgirls, reactions to
        breakthrough, 44–49
    unawareness of Negro
        dissatisfaction, 70–71

DATE DUE

MAY 2			
GAYLORD			PRINTED IN U.S.A.